SKILLS FOR SUCCESS

SKILL-BUILDING SCIENCE

GRADES 5-6

by Jennifer Linrud Sinsel

Carson-Dellosa Publishing Company, Inc.
Greensboro, North Carolina

CREDITS

EDITOR: Matthew Fisher

LAYOUT DESIGN: Van Harris

INSIDE ILLUSTRATIONS: Jenny Campbell

COVER DESIGN: Matthew Van Zomeren

COVER PHOTOS: © Comstock, Inc.
© Photodisc
Photo courtesy of NASA

ISBN 1-59441-218-9

TABLE OF CONTENTS

TABLE OF CONTENTS

INTRODUCTION

When asked to characterize a scientist, most students will describe a funny little man in glasses and a white coat, spending his days isolated in a lab with test tubes and brightly colored chemicals. As teachers, it is our responsibility to change this perception—to convince every child that he is actually a scientist. In fact, anyone who has ever solved a problem, struggled to understand something about his environment, asked a question, or remained skeptical about an answer is practicing science.

This book is intended to foster these qualities, as well as the natural curiosity children have about the world around them, by reinforcing and enriching the concepts taught in a fifth- and sixth-grade science curriculum. Each activity is designed to pique student interest in the chosen topic through hands-on activities, critical-thinking exercises, engineering challenges, and student-designed experiments. Many activities are self-guided, so students can complete them with little teacher assistance.

The book is divided into three sections: Physical Science, Earth Science, and Life Science. The categories within each section follow the fundamental concepts and principles outlined in the content areas of the National Science Education Standards. Embedded within these categories are lessons and activities designed with the standards in mind, including activities in guided inquiry, technology, science in society, and the history and nature of science. Furthermore, Science Skills pages help reinforce crucial skills necessary to engage in learning and doing science. A description of each section is given below.

Science Skills—These activities reinforce the skills necessary to conduct scientific investigations. Skills covered include measuring, converting metric units, timing, making models, observing, graphing, making inferences, and several others.

Experimental Design—The National Science Education Standards list "science as inquiry" as one of the content standards. The Experimental Design activities in this book align with this standard.

Engineering Challenge—The National Science Education Standards list "science and technology" as one of the content standards. The Engineering Challenge activities in this book align with this standard.

Science in Society—The National Science Education Standards list "science in personal and social perspectives" as one of the content standards. The Science in Society activities in this book align with this standard.

Spotlight on Scientists—The National Science Education Standards list "history and nature of science" as one of the content standards. Each Spotlight on Scientists page in this book includes a short biography of a scientist who works in an applicable field. A short activity or writing assignment accompanies each scientist's biography.

The "Write" Stuff—Good writing skills are essential in any profession, but most scientists will agree that they are especially important when communicating scientific findings. These activities will encourage and reinforce both creative and scientific writing skills.

Just the Facts—These reproducible worksheets provide factual information and review basic concepts required to conduct activities.

A GUIDE TO EXPERIMENTAL DESIGN

When scientists see something they do not understand, they try to find out more about it. Scientific knowledge requires evidence. That evidence is gained by conducting experiments. The scientific method is a guide to performing experiments and is one way to organize the information that is gathered. Although there is not a right way to study something, some ways are better than others. This introduction to experimental design using the scientific method will help you and your students create your own science investigations, one step at a time.

The National Science Education Standards require that students at these grade levels have the understanding and ability to complete a scientific inquiry. The variety of activities in this book can be used as stepping stones to provide students with basic background knowledge, experience, and the confidence needed to develop their own independent scientific inquiries.

A **Sample Experiment**, which can be used in several ways, is provided for each Experimental Design activity. The Sample Experiment:

- may be followed step-by-step to help students develop an understanding of the scientific inquiry process.
- may be used as reference to guide students toward the development of an inquiry that is identical to the sample experiment.
- may be used as an example or demonstration for students before they develop their own original inquiries.

The sample experiment is just that—a sample of the hundreds of scientific inquiries that can be developed around each concept. Encourage students to make observations about the world around them. From these observations, students can develop questions and conduct inquiries. (Additional inquiry questions can also be found on the Internet.) The following pages will help you guide students through the process of scientific inquiry.

THE SCIENTIFIC METHOD

1. OBSERVE: Use the five senses to examine the world around you.
2. QUESTION: Ask a scientific question about the observations.
3. RESEARCH: Find information about the topic of the question.
4. HYPOTHESIZE: Write what you think will happen.
5. EXPERIMENT: List materials, write a procedure, and conduct the experiment.
   - VARIABLES, CONTROL, AND CONSTANTS: Define what will be tested.
   - RECORD DATA: Write information (measurements) on a data table.
   - GRAPH DATA: Create a picture of the gathered data.
6. COMPARE RESULTS: Summarize what happened.
7. CONCLUDE: Decide what it all means.

A GUIDE TO EXPERIMENTAL DESIGN

1. OBSERVE: Science begins and ends with observation and has observations throughout it! Scientists are trained observers. **Observations** are things noticed using the five senses—sight, hearing, taste, touch, and smell. As students work on experiments, help them train themselves to notice even the slightest changes. A good scientist carefully observes everything about an experiment and records those observations on a data table.

2. QUESTION: First, the student must create a **question** that will form the basis for a hypothesis. However, if the question can be answered with yes or no, it is not a good topic. For example, a student may choose the question "Does my little sister like broccoli?" A better question might be "How can broccoli be served so that five-year-old children will eat it?" Guide the student to understand that the second question cannot be answered with a yes or no. To find the answer, several five-year-old children could be served broccoli that has been prepared in different ways.

3. RESEARCH: Next, the student must gather information from different sources to learn more about the topic. For example, if the student's topic is the effect of adding fertilizer to the soil of tulips, she will need to learn about tulips, including the kind of soil the plants prefer and how much water and sunlight they need. Have the student spend time observing tulips and writing observations based on things noticed with her senses.

4. HYPOTHESIZE: A **hypothesis** is a speculative statement that proposes a possible explanation to some occurrence or event. Based on previous scientific knowledge or research, it states what the scientist thinks will happen in the experiment. The student should phrase the hypothesis as an "If . . . then . . ." sentence. "If (independent variable) affects (dependent variable), then (your prediction) will happen."

5. EXPERIMENT: A basic introduction to the concepts of writing a procedure and defining controls, constants, and variables in a scientific inquiry is presented in the Controls and Variables activity (page 86). It may be helpful to complete this activity before any Experimental Design activities.

VARIABLES, CONTROLS, AND CONSTANTS:

After the hypothesis is written, the variables must be defined. A **variable** is anything that could change in the experiment. However, a scientist will change only one variable to see how it impacts the thing he is studying. The **independent variable** is the one thing that the scientist changes in the experiment. Every other variable must remain the same. The variables that must not change are called **constants**.

When one factor (the independent variable) is changed, the scientist will watch what happens. What happens is called the **dependent variable**.

The student must also include a group of test subjects to demonstrate how the experiment works when the independent variable is not applied. This is known as the **control group**. The group of test subjects that is used to show what happens when the independent variable is applied is called the **experimental group**. The student should record the results from the control and experimental groups on the same data table. Then, it will be easy to compare the groups to see what changes are caused by the independent variable.

A GUIDE TO EXPERIMENTAL DESIGN

MATERIALS: A student should list all of the materials that are needed for the experiment. This list should be checked by the teacher prior to the student beginning the experiment.

- Have students include exact measurements on their materials lists. For example, instead of writing "water," a student should specify "100 milliliters of water."
- Measuring tools should be part of the materials list. Remind students that in science experiments, all measurements should be metric, so all measuring tools should have metric increments.
- Have students list any needed safety equipment. Most experiments require goggles. Chemicals require a chemical apron and gloves. Heat requires hot pads. Students should be properly trained to work with open flames, stoves, or other electric appliances prior to their use in an experiment.
- Students should make sure they have gathered enough materials for several trials of the experiments.
- If any living test subjects are required, permission must be obtained in advance.

PROCEDURE: When a student begins to write her **procedure**, emphasize that the experiment must be explained in a step-by-step format exactly as it will be conducted. Another student should be able to follow the steps and complete the experiment in exactly the same way. That is how scientists check each other's work. If another student can repeat the experiment and get the same results, then the procedure was explained well. Explain that after trying an experiment, another person might want to build on the first person's research. Each researcher who studies a topic adds little bits and pieces to the understanding of the topic until amazing things are discovered.

PROCEDURE EXAMPLE

Clear Procedure:

1. Place 10 cm of soil at the bottom of each of the four pots.
2. Place one tulip bulb in the center of each pot.
3. Cover each bulb with 10 cm of soil.
4. Carefully pour 10 mL of liquid fertilizer into three of the tulip pots.
5. Slowly water each pot with 20 mL of water each day.

Unclear Procedure:

1. Put some soil in the pots.
2. Put the bulbs in the pots.
3. Cover the bulbs with soil.
4. Pour a little bit of fertilizer into some of the tulip pots.
5. Water the bulbs.

MEASURING DATA: All experiments produce data. **Data** are the results of the experiment and should be written on a chart or graph to clearly show how they were measured. The results should be quantified by measuring a specific factor, such as time, temperature, volume, height, weight, mass, etc.

It is important that students plan how the results will be measured before they start their experiments. The way data is measured will be determined by the way an experiment is performed. The results will also need to be recorded over the length of the experiment.

DATA TABLE EXAMPLE

	Average Height of Tulips in Centimeters	
Date	Experimental Group	Control Group
3/25	10 cm	10 cm
3/26	12 cm	11 cm
3/27	15 cm	12 cm

RECORDING DATA: During the experiment, students will write information on a **data table**. The data table should provide a detailed heading for each column and row. Make sure students also record the units in which the data was measured.

GRAPHING DATA: An important part of a science inquiry is creating a **graph**, or picture of the data, that will explain the data to other scientists. Tell students that the type of graph they use depends on the type of data they have collected.

Bar graphs are used to compare quantities that are not continually changing. For example, a bar graph can be used to compare the heights of four people. The **independent variable** is always placed on the x-axis (horizontal axis). Then, the **scale** is chosen by looking at the highest and lowest measurements of the heights of the four people and written on the y-axis (vertical axis). In the tulip example (above), a bar graph could be used to show the final height of each tulip.

Line graphs are used to show how one variable in an experiment responds to the change in another. Pairs of numbers are used to express a relationship between the dependent and independent variables. In a line graph, the **independent variable** is placed on the x-axis and the **dependent variable** on the y-axis. Explain that line graphs are most often used when they can help determine the accuracy of the hypothesis by showing patterns in the data. In the tulip example (above), the line graph could show a picture of how the independent variable (addition of fertilizer) affected the dependent variable (height of the tulips).

After the data points have been plotted on the graph, do not allow students to connect the dots of the line graph! Instead, have them draw a line (or curve) that follows the data as closely as possible, without actually connecting the dots. Doing this shows the trend that the data suggests.

6. **COMPARE RESULTS:** After several trials have been conducted, what happened in the experiment should be clear. These are the **results**. Students can explain the results to others through the data shown in a graph or table. Only a simple, factual summary of what happened in the experiment needs to be written.

7. **CONCLUDE:** Students should ask, "What happened? What went right? What went wrong? What would I do differently next time? What did I learn?" This conclusion is not the same as the data or the results. The **conclusion** is a student's opinion and observations about the results and the data that was collected.

NAME ______________________ DATE __________

QUESTION:

Ask a **question** that will form the basis for your hypothesis.

HYPOTHESIS:

Write what you think will happen in the experiment. The **hypothesis** should be stated as an "If . . . then . . ." sentence. "If (independent variable) affects (dependent variable), then (your prediction) will happen."

If ______________________________,

then ______________________________.

VARIABLES, CONTROL, AND CONSTANTS:

What is the **independent variable** in this experiment?

What is the **dependent variable** in this experiment?

What is the **control** group?

What variables are the **constants**?

NAME ______________________ DATE __________

____

MATERIALS: List the materials here. (Include safety equipment.)

- ______________
- ______________
- ______________
- ______________
- ______________
- ______________
- ______________
- ______________
- ______________
- ______________
- ______________
- ______________

Decide what you will measure and explain how you will measure it.

____

____

PROCEDURE: Write the steps for the experiment. Explain what you will do and exactly how you will complete each step. Number each step. If you need more space, continue the steps on another piece of paper.

____

____

____

____

____

____

____

____

____

____

____

NAME ______________________ DATE ______________

DATA TABLE: Write your observations or data in the table below. Remember to label the measurements with the units you used.

GRAPH: On the graph paper on page 14, create a graph that shows a picture of the data you collected in this experiment.

RESULTS: After you have conducted several trials of your experiment, you will know what happened in the experiment. These are your results. You can explain them to other people through the data you show in a graph or table.

1. When you applied the independent variable, what happened to the dependent variable?

2. Write a brief summary of the experiment's results.

NAME ____________________ DATE ____________

CONCLUSION: What happened? What went right? What went wrong? What would you do differently next time? What did you learn? The conclusion is your opinion and observations about the experiment's results and the data you collected.

1. Were your results the same each time?

2. Is there anything else that could have caused the change you observed?

3. Did you have any problems? Explain them. How would you correct these problems in the future?

4. What would you change to make the experiment better?

5. Explain how your results were different from what you expected.

6. Write at least two new questions you have now that your experiment is finished.

NAME ____________________ DATE ____________

TITLE: ______________________________

y-axis: ____________________ (dependent variable)

x-axis: ____________________
(independent variable)

GRAPH KEY

☐ ____________________ ☐ ____________________

☐ ____________________ ☐ ____________________

☐ ____________________ ☐ ____________________

Observing Polymers (page 18)

Cornstarch and water make a fascinating (and messy!) natural polymer. This mixture has pressure-dependent viscosity. This means the more pressure you exert on it, the less it flows. You can pick up the mixture by squeezing it, but if you let it sit in your hand, it will drip out like a liquid. Be aware that after some time the mixture will dry out and the cornstarch powder may make a mess.

Create Your Own Polymers! (page 20)

Borax is sold in stores as a laundry detergent. It is important to label any solution containing borax. Once you use a container for borax solution, do not use it for anything else. Even after cleaning the container, borax will contaminate materials put into the container for a long time because it is very alkaline.

Before the activity, prepare a borax solution for students by mixing 1/8 cup (29.6 mL) of borax laundry detergent into 2 cups (0.5 L) of warm water. Shake until most of the borax dissolves. Allow the solution to cool. This will produce enough borax solution for several classes of students.

The glue and the borax solution may be stored separately in 2-ounce plastic cups or ramekins. These may be purchased at school supply, craft, or food stores. Ramekins with lids work especially well because ingredients may be portioned before the activity and then stacked.

There are many combinations that will create polymers. Have students work in groups of four as they experiment using different amounts of the ingredients. Encourage them to conduct research on the Internet to find other combinations of these materials to create other polymers.

The following formula will produce a slime-like polymer:

1. In a clear cup, place 2 tablespoons (29.57 mL) of glue. Add 4 tablespoons (59.15 mL) of water to the glue. Stir.
2. Add 2–3 drops of food coloring.
3. Add 1 tablespoon (14.79 mL) of borax solution to the glue solution. Gently stir the mixture with a stirring stick. If there is some remaining water or glue, add another tablespoon of borax solution.
4. Remove the polymer from the cup and let it ooze between your fingers. Place it on an object, such as a bottle or a rock, and watch it ooze down the sides!

The following formula will produce a bouncy ball-like polymer:

1. In a clear cup, place 2 tablespoons (29.57 mL) of glue.
2. Add 2–3 drops of food coloring.
3. Add 3 tablespoons (44.37 mL) of borax solution to the glue. Then, gently stir the mixture with a stirring stick. If there is some remaining water or glue, add another tablespoon of borax solution.
4. Remove the polymer from the cup and roll it between your hands into a ball shape. After a few minutes, try bouncing the ball on the floor.

Students may take their polymers home in resealable plastic bags. Remind students to be careful with these polymers. They may stain carpets and clothing. Also, because these types of polymers may clog drains, do not allow the disposal of unused polymers down any drain.

Solutes and Solvents (page 22)

Caution: Before completing any food activity, ask families' permission and inquire about students' food allergies and religious or other food preferences.

A Sweet Solution (page 23)

Caution: Remind students to use caution when handling hot liquids and using heating equipment, such as hot plates.

Newton's First Law (page 29)

Caution: Before completing this activity, ask families about possible latex allergies. Also, remember that uninflated or popped balloons may present a choking hazard. Students should use caution when using hot glue guns.

The glue must make a complete seal between the push-pull sports cap and the compact disc. A 12" (30.48 cm) balloon works well for this activity and will provide enough air to maintain the hovercraft's movement for about 30 seconds.

Newton's First Law (continued)

If the fully inflated balloon is too heavy and drags on the table, have students push the balloon farther down onto the cap, closer to the compact disc.

Collect free promotional compact discs from Internet service providers for this activity.

Newton's Third Law (page 32)

Film canisters can be obtained from a local photography lab. Determine the number of film canisters you need to complete the activity. A few days prior to the activity, ask a lab technician to save that many canisters for you.

Highway Crash Cushions (page 33)

Caution: Before completing this activity, ask families about possible latex allergies. Also, remember that uninflated or popped balloons may present a choking hazard.

Caution: Raw or lightly cooked eggs may be contaminated with salmonella, a bacteria responsible for food poisoning. To prevent illness from bacteria, use only properly refrigerated, clean, sound-shelled, fresh, grade AA or A eggs.

Simulate the materials used in crash cushions with the following materials:

Shredded rubber tires: Fill the plastic container with rubber bands.

Water barrels: Fill three balloons with water.

Aluminum barrels: Crumple pieces of aluminum foil.

Balloon-Powered Cars (page 34)

A simple balloon-powered car can be constructed by using the plastic foam tray as the car's carriage. Attach two straws to the underside of the tray with tape. Thread a washer on each end of both straws for the wheels. Fully inflate the balloon and secure with a binder clip. Put a piece of tape on the bottom of the balloon and attach it to the top of the carriage, with the balloon's opening facing the rear of the car. Remove the binder clip to make the car move.

The Metric System (page 40)

Students should have a basic knowledge of the metric system and how to perform unit conversions before completing this activity. A metric conversion chart is provided at the top of the page.

Conductors and Insulators (page 41)

Students should create a device that will allow an electrical current to flow from the 6-volt battery to the flashlight bulb. Prepare three wires (A, B, and C) before class by stripping 2" (5.08 cm) of the insulation from each end of the wires.

Students may follow these steps to create a complete electrical circuit.

1. Connect wire A to one terminal of the battery.
2. Connect wire B to the other terminal.
3. Then, connect both wire C and the other end of the wire B to the flashlight bulb. Use a small piece of electrical tape to hold these wires in place.
4. Connect the other end of wire C to wire A to complete the circuit. The flashlight bulb should light.
5. To test items for the activity, simply disconnect wire A and wire C and place the item within the circuit. If the item is a conductor, the flashlight bulb will light when the circuit is complete. If the item is an insulator, the flashlight bulb will not light.

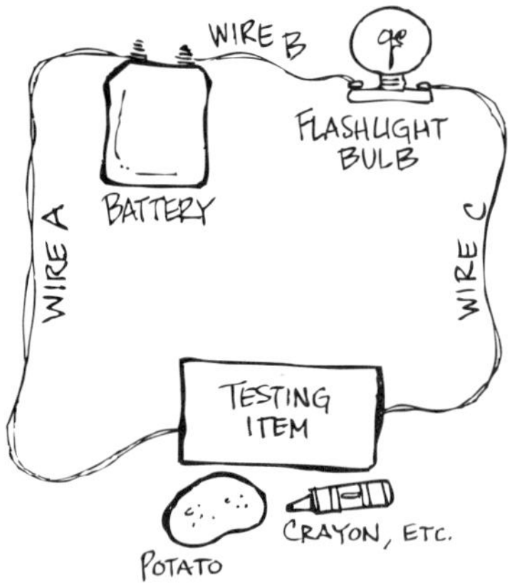

Fast-Food Frenzy (page 43)

Caution: Students should use caution when using hot glue guns.

POLYMERS

JUST THE FACTS

What do a balloon, a piece of paper, and a compact disc have in common? Each is made of repeating units that are so small we cannot see them without a microscope. Scientists call objects made of repeating units **polymers.**

A polymer is like a long chain of paper clips, and each paper clip is a molecule. Several paper clips linked together represents a polymer. Polymers are usually very flexible and stretchable. Some common examples of materials made from polymers are plastic bottles, garbage bags, chewing gum, and plastic foam.

Examine the list of objects below. Circle the objects that you think are made of polymers.

newspaper	tree branch	copper penny	human hair
tortoise shell	pencil eraser	crackers	disposable diaper
plastic foam plates	sugar	leather	glass bottle
salt	egg carton	plastic bag	beef jerky

Use science books, magazines, encyclopedias, or the Internet to research other types of polymers we use every day. Then, make a collage using pictures or drawings of these objects and present your findings to the class.

TRY THIS! One way to demonstrate how polymers behave requires a few of your classmates to help you out. For this activity, pretend you are a molecule. Find two more "molecules" and grab hands to form a three-person chain. You have now created a polymer. Continue to add students to your chain to make a longer polymer.

Begin walking at a normal pace, keeping your hands linked. Notice that as you walk, your chain begins to stretch out. Also notice that the person at the end of the chain may not always be traveling in the same direction as the person at the beginning of the chain. This demonstrates the polymer's flexibility.

NAME______________________________ DATE______________

OBSERVING POLYMERS

SCIENCE SKILLS

A scientific experiment begins with a scientist asking a question about something that she observes. These observations are usually based on what she might see, hear, smell, touch, and taste—her senses. In this activity, you will practice your **observation skills** as you use several common household items to make your own polymer.

MATERIALS:

- cornstarch
- coins
- measuring cup
- pie tin or plastic food container
- food coloring
- toothpicks
- water
- paper clips
- craft stick

PROCEDURE

1. Pour 1 cup (24 mL) of water into the container.
2. Add a few drops of food coloring and stir the water with the craft stick so that the color distributes evenly.
3. Add 2 cups (47 mL) of cornstarch a little at a time, kneading it slowly with your hands. The substance will become thick and hard to mix, but keep at it!
4. When the cornstarch is mixed in, you will have created some ooze—a polymer!

OBSERVATIONS: Caution: Do not put this polymer in your mouth.

1. What does it feel like when you rest your hand on top of the polymer? ______________________

____

____

2. What does it look like? ____

____

____

3. What does it sound like when you squeeze it in your hand? ______________________

____

____

On another piece of paper, answer the following questions in complete sentences.

4. What happens when you quickly rub your finger across the top of the polymer?
5. What happens when you squeeze some of the polymer in your hand?
6. Does the heat from your hands affect the polymer? How can you prove or disprove this?
7. What kinds of objects float in the polymer? What kinds of objects sink?
8. Is your polymer a liquid or a solid? Can you prove it?

NAME________________________________ DATE____________

POLYMER POND CREATURES

THE "WRITE" STUFF

PHYSICAL SCIENCE

Scientists have discovered a new island in a remote part of the Pacific Ocean. You have been asked to accompany an expedition to examine the creatures that live there. Everyone is particularly interested in a pond of ooze located near the center of the island. The pond of ooze is very similar to the cornstarch and water polymer you created in the Observing Polymers activity (page 18). Keep your observations of this polymer in mind as you write a description of the creatures that might live in the pond of ooze.

- What do they look like?
- How do they prevent themselves from getting stuck?
- What other special challenges do they face because of their environment?
- What do they eat?
- Do they have any natural predators?
- Would scientists be interested in studying them? Why or why not?
- On another piece of paper, draw the creatures and label their body parts.

NAME_______________________ DATE_______________

CREATE YOUR OWN POLYMERS!

ENGINEERING CHALLENGE

Have you ever wondered how things we use every day are invented and manufactured? Materials like plastic are so common that we do not usually give their origins a second thought. However, plastics and other polymers exist because scientists called **chemical engineers** invent new materials and find new ways to use them.

CHALLENGE: Create a flexible or elastic polymer.

MATERIALS:

- white school glue
- borax solution
- food coloring
- paper towels
- graduated cylinders or beakers
- measuring spoons
- small plastic cups
- water
- stirring stick
- resealable plastic bags

GUIDELINES

1. Using different combinations of water, borax solution, white glue, and food coloring, create a formula for a flexible and elastic polymer.
2. As you attempt to create a polymer, record the amount of each ingredient you use in the data tables below and on page 21 so that you do not repeat incorrect combinations. There are several versions of polymers that can be made using these materials.
3. After each trial, record the observations of the combination of ingredients on the data table.
4. If the first trial does not create a flexible and elastic polymer, alter the amount of one ingredient and try again!

DATA TABLE 1: Remember to label each measurement with the unit you used.

Ingredients Used	Amount	Observations	
Water		Physical Appearance	
White Glue		Texture	
Food Coloring		Other Observations	
Borax Solution			

NAME ______________________________ DATE ______________

DATA TABLE 2: Remember to label each measurement with the unit you used.

Ingredients Used	Amount	Observations	
Water		Physical Appearance	
White Glue		Texture	
Food Coloring		Other Observations	
Borax Solution			

DATA TABLE 3: Remember to label each measurement with the unit you used.

Ingredients Used	Amount	Observations	
Water		Physical Appearance	
White Glue		Texture	
Food Coloring		Other Observations	
Borax Solution			

RESULTS: Answer the following questions in complete sentences on another piece of paper.

1. Describe what happened when the glue was combined with the water.
2. Describe what happened when the glue and water mixture was combined with the borax solution.
3. There are many possible combinations of these materials that can create polymers. Why do you think each of your polymers was different?

TRY THIS! Choose one of the polymers that you created. Think about what it might be used for and who might buy it. Write a script for a one minute commercial that will deliver an important message to people about why they should purchase the polymer. Then, use a video camera or tape recorder to record the commercial and share it with the class.

NAME________________________ DATE____________

SOLUTES AND SOLVENTS

JUST THE FACTS

Have you ever noticed that powdered drink mix in a pitcher seems to disappear after you pour water into it? Although it looks like it has mysteriously vanished, the drink mix has simply dissolved in the water and become part of a **solution**.

A solution has two parts, a solute and a solvent. The **solute** is the substance being dissolved. The **solvent** is the substance into which the solute is dissolved. In the powdered drink mix example above, the powdered drink mix is the solute and the water is the solvent. In this activity, you will experience the dissolving process firsthand—in a very tasty way!

QUESTION: Which is the fastest method of dissolving a small piece of chocolate in your mouth?

MATERIALS:

- 3 individually wrapped chocolates
- stopwatch or clock with a second hand

PROCEDURE

1. Unwrap the first piece of chocolate. Place it in your mouth, but do not chew it or stir it around with your tongue. Record how long it takes for the chocolate to completely dissolve.
2. Unwrap and place the second piece of chocolate in your mouth. This time, stir it around with your tongue. Record how long it takes the chocolate to completely dissolve.
3. Unwrap and place the third piece of chocolate in your mouth and chew it. Record how long it takes the chocolate to completely dissolve.

DATA TABLE: Remember to label each measurement with the unit you used.

	No Movement	Stirring	Chewing
Time Needed to Dissolve			

THINK ABOUT THIS! Answer the following questions in complete sentences on another piece of paper.

1. What was the fastest way to make the chocolate dissolve?
2. Why do you think this way worked faster than the others?
3. Name the solute and solvent in this experiment.
4. Name the solute and solvent in the following solutions:

   a. salt water b. soft drink c. chocolate milk d. instant coffee

A SWEET SOLUTION SAMPLE EXPERIMENT

QUESTION: How does the temperature of a solvent affect the rate of dissolution of a solute?

HYPOTHESIS: If the temperature of a solvent affects the rate at which a solute will dissolve, then a solute will dissolve faster in a solvent with a higher temperature.

VARIABLES, CONTROL, AND CONSTANTS:

Independent variable: Temperature of the solvent

Dependent variable: Amount of time needed for the solute to dissolve completely

Control: A solute in a room temperature solvent

Constants: Variables that must remain the same

- type and amount of solvent
- type and amount of solute
- method of heating and cooling solvent
- method of timing dissolution rate
- type of thermometer
- type of container

MATERIALS:

- water
- 9 sugar cubes
- 3 scientific thermometers
- 4 beakers
- stirring stick
- stopwatch
- hot plate
- beaker tongs
- water pitcher
- refrigerator
- safety goggles

PROCEDURE

1. One day before conducting the experiment, fill a pitcher with water and place it in the refrigerator.
2. Fill the first beaker with 100 mL of the refrigerated water.
3. Fill another beaker with 200 mL of water and place it on the hot plate. Place a thermometer in the beaker. Heat the water to 140°F (60°C). Use the beaker tongs to carefully pour 100 mL of this hot water into the second beaker.
4. Fill the third beaker with 100 mL of room temperature water.
5. Place a thermometer in each beaker and record the temperature of the water in each beaker on the data table.
6. Place one sugar cube in each beaker.
7. Every two minutes, use the stirring stick to stir the water and sugar cube in each beaker three times.
8. Record the temperature of the water in each beaker every minute until the sugar cube in that beaker completely dissolves.
9. Record the time it takes for each sugar cube to completely dissolve in the hot, cold, and room temperature water.
10. Repeat steps 2–9 two additional times. Find the average rate of dissolution of the sugar cubes in each temperature of water. Record it on the data table.

PHYSICAL SCIENCE

NAME______________________________DATE______________

A SWEET SOLUTION

EXPERIMENTAL DESIGN

A **solution** has two parts, a solute and a solvent. The **solute** is the substance being dissolved. The **solvent** is the substance into which the solute is dissolved. You can find examples of solutions all around you in your everyday life, such as salt water, coffee, and chocolate milk.

TASK: Design an experiment to determine the fastest way to dissolve a sugar cube in water. Complete the worksheets (pages 10–14) as you design and perform your Sweet Solution experiment.

HINTS

HYPOTHESIS:

- Think about what you already know about solutes and solvents, based on what you learned in the Solutes and Solvents activity (page 22).

VARIABLES, CONTROL, AND CONSTANTS:

- What will you test?
- What will change as a result of the independent variable?
- To which trial will you compare all of the results?
- Which parts of the experiment must stay the same?

GRAPH:

- Create a graph that shows a picture of the data you collected in this experiment. Remember to label both axes and give the graph an appropriate title.

NAME______________________________________DATE______________

MEET DANA HAMILTON

SPOTLIGHT ON SCIENTISTS

PHYSICAL SCIENCE

Have you ever wondered what happens to water that goes down the drain from your sink, shower, or toilet? It simply seems to disappear, which is very convenient for most of us! However, some scientists have the important job of testing the water that goes through our sewer systems to make sure it is cleaned properly before being released back into natural bodies of water, such as lakes and ponds.

Dana Hamilton is a **field chemist** who works for the water department in Wichita, Kansas. Her job is to check the sewer lines downstream from area restaurants for large amounts of grease. Restaurants that pour too much grease into their sewer lines must install special plumbing fixtures to stop grease from reaching the public sewer system. Ms. Hamilton cares about the environment. This concern is the main reason she decided to enter the field of water contamination and treatment. She is the only person in Wichita who tests for food grease in sewer lines, which makes her unique in her field!

Look at the following list of materials and describe how each of them could find its way into the sewer system.

1. Shampoo ______________________________
2. Soap ______________________________
3. Mouthwash ______________________________
4. Motor oil ______________________________
5. Lawn care chemicals ______________________________
6. Leaves ______________________________
7. Kitchen cleaners ______________________________
8. Gum wrappers ______________________________
9. Toothpaste ______________________________
10. Leftover food ______________________________

TRY THIS: On another piece of paper, describe how each item on the list above affects the water in the sewer system. Describe how people can prevent these materials from entering the water supply.

OIL AND WATER DON'T MIX!

SCIENCE IN SOCIETY

Although we do not often consider it, oil is a part of daily life. It is used in the gasoline needed to fuel cars and can be used to make the plastic in food containers, picnic ware, soft drink bottles, toys, and many other items. Society is truly dependent on oil and its products.

However, it is the environment that often pays the price for these luxuries. In 1989, the oil tanker *Exxon Valdez* ran aground off the coast of Alaska, spilling 11 million gallons of oil into the ocean. This amount of oil would fill 125 Olympic-size swimming pools! Although this spill is not the largest in history, it is often considered the most damaging to the environment. Thousands of birds and mammals along the coast of Alaska were affected, and many did not survive. Even many years later, the populations of some of the affected species have still not fully recovered. Many volunteers took on the difficult job of cleaning the animals that were coated with oil. To get an idea of the challenge these volunteers faced, try the following activity.

MATERIALS:

- water (warm and cold)
- white feathers (available in craft stores)
- vegetable oil
- cocoa powder
- 4 plastic bowls
- dishwashing detergent
- graduated cylinder
- measuring spoon
- plastic cup
- paper towels
- plastic spoon
- magnifying glass

PROCEDURE

1. Examine a feather with a magnifying glass. On another piece of paper, draw how the feather is shaped.
2. Fill one bowl with water to 2" (5.08 cm) below the rim. Dip the feather in water for one minute. Examine the feather again and draw any differences. Allow the feather to dry.
3. Pour 10 mL of vegetable oil into the plastic cup. Add 1 tbsp (29.57 mL) of cocoa powder to the vegetable oil. Stir with the plastic spoon. This will represent crude oil that may be released in an ocean oil spill.
4. Pour the oil and cocoa mixture into the bowl of water.
5. Dip three feathers into the oil on the surface of the water for one minute.
6. Remove the feathers from the oil. Place them on a paper towel. Use the magnifying glass to examine the feathers. Draw how the feathers look after they have been dipped in oil.
7. Try three methods of cleaning the feathers.
   a) Cold water washing: Pour cold water into a bowl. Try washing an oily feather.
   b) Warm water washing: Pour warm water into a bowl. Try washing an oily feather.
   c) Washing with detergent: Pour warm water and 2 tbsp (29.57 mL) of dishwashing detergent into a bowl. Try washing an oily feather.

TRY THIS! On another piece of paper, write what you learned about cleaning feathers that are coated with oil. How could someone use what you learned in the real world?

NAME____DATE______________

READING AND MAKING GRAPHS

SCIENCE SKILLS

Scientists often share the results of their experiments with other scientists through the use of graphs. As a student scientist, it is important to be able to make and read graphs so that you can effectively share your data with others. Although there are many different types of graphs, this activity concentrates on the two most common—**bar graphs** and **line graphs**.

Look at the following graphs and answer the questions below.

Bar Graph	Line Graph
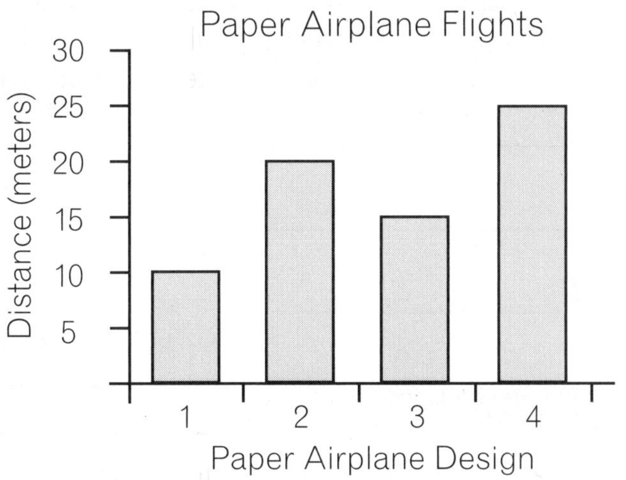	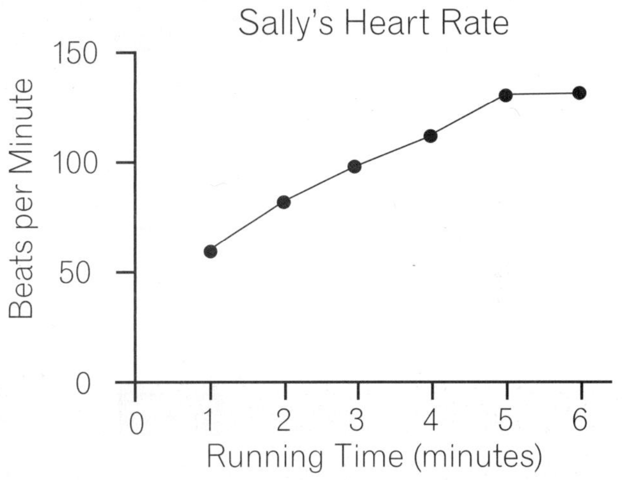

BAR GRAPH

1. How many meters did Design 1 fly? ______________________________

2. Which paper airplane flew the shortest distance? ______________________________

3. How many designs of paper airplanes were tested? ______________________________

4. Based on the data, explain which paper airplane design flew the furthest.

____

____

LINE GRAPH

5. At how many minutes did Sally's heart rate increase to 100 beats per minute? ____________

6. How long did it take for Sally's heart rate to become constant? ______________________

7. According to the graph, what was Sally's peak heart rate? ______________________

8. Predict what Sally's heart rate will be at seven minutes. ______________________

NAME ________________________ DATE ____________

PHYSICAL SCIENCE

TRY THIS! Notice that each graph shows a different type of data. Bar graphs are used when one of the axes displays objects, such as designs of paper airplanes. Line graphs are used when both axes display figures, such as times or rates. Now it is your turn!

Make graphs to display the following data. For each data set, decide if you should use a bar graph or a line graph.

DATA SET 1: Benjamin wanted to know which amount of sugar added to one cup of water will create the longest rock candy sugar crystals. He tested four different amounts of sugar in four separate cups of water. The data table below shows the data from his experiment.

Amount of Sugar	Length of Rock Candy Crystals
1 cup	3 cm
$1\frac{1}{2}$ cups	5 cm
2 cups	7 cm
$2\frac{1}{2}$ cups	14 cm

DATA SET 2: Amy wanted to find out which type of light allows a plant to grow the tallest. She grew three plants, each under a different type of light. She measured the plants at the same time every day. The data table below shows the data from the plant that was grown in direct sunlight.

Day	Height of Plant
1	2 cm
2	2 cm
3	2.5 cm
4	3 cm
5	4 cm
6	5.5 cm
7	7 cm

NEWTON'S FIRST LAW

JUST THE FACTS

A long time ago, a scientist named Sir Isaac Newton researched **forces** and **motion**. After conducting experiments over many years, he came up with three laws describing the way objects move and the forces that act on them. We still use his ideas today to explain why things move the way they do, especially when it comes to complicated ideas like spaceflight!

Newton's first law states that objects that are not moving will stay still unless something else moves them. It also says that objects that are moving will continue to move in a straight line unless something else stops them or changes their direction.

You will create a model that demonstrates Newton's first law. Follow the directions below to make a hovercraft. Then, observe how different forces affect the hovercraft's movement.

PHYSICAL SCIENCE

MATERIALS:

- compact disc
- push-pull sports cap from a plastic water bottle
- 12" (30.48 cm) balloon
- hot glue gun
- glue sticks
- large book

PROCEDURE

1. Use the hot glue gun to attach the push-pull sports cap to the center of the compact disc so that the cap is facing up. Allow to dry. You have made a hovercraft.

2. Put the hovercraft on a tabletop. Make sure the cap on the hovercraft is closed. Inflate the balloon and twist it closed. (Do not tie it.) Attach the balloon to the cap Then, untwist the balloon. The hovercraft should not move. **This demonstrates the first part of Newton's first law:** objects that are not moving will stay still unless something else moves them.

3. Flick the hovercraft with your fingers so that it moves. You provided the force necessary to get an object moving, which demonstrates the **second part of Newton's first law**. (The hovercraft probably did not go very far.)
4. Open the cap so that air from the balloon can escape. Your hovercraft may move a little on its own.
5. Apply force to the hovercraft by flicking it with your fingers again. If your hovercraft has been assembled correctly, it should zoom across the table!

6. Place a book upright on the table and flick the hovercraft toward it at an angle. Notice that the hovercraft will generally move in a straight line until it hits the book, which causes it to change direction. **This demonstrates the third part of Newton's first law.**

7. Play with the hovercraft until you have a good idea about how different forces affect the hovercraft's movement.

NAME ______________________ DATE ______________

Now that you have some understanding of **Newton's first law**, you should be aware of some other terminology that goes along with it. First, let's see how well you remember the first law. In your own words, write Newton's first law on the lines below:

____

____

Another name for Newton's first law is the **law of inertia**. **Inertia** is the tendency of an object to keep doing what it is doing. In other words, if an object is sitting still, it will stay in the same place until something moves it. If it is moving, it will keep moving until something stops it. Does this sound familiar to you?

It is very hard to change the motion of an object with lots of inertia (an avalanche, a linebacker, etc.). It is usually easy to change the motion of an object with little inertia (a mosquito, a watermelon seed, etc.). Remember, an object's inertia is not always dependent on its size—a baseball is a tiny object, but it has a lot of inertia when being thrown by a professional pitcher!

1. Name several objects with a lot of inertia: ______________________

   ____

2. Name several objects with a little inertia: ______________________

   ____

3. Does the hovercraft have more inertia when it is at rest or when it is moving? Explain.

   ____

   ____

You may have noticed that part of Newton's first law does not seem to make sense. If a moving object stays moving until something stops it, then what causes the hovercraft to eventually stop? Newton said that a moving object will stop moving when some force acts on it. The force in this case is called friction. **Friction** is the push two objects give when they rub against each other. Try rubbing your hands together. The heat you feel is caused by the friction of two objects (your hands) rubbing against each other.

4. Name the two objects creating friction to make the hovercraft stop moving.

   ____

5. When the hovercraft moves, is there more or less friction between it and the table? Why?

   ____

TRY THIS! Is there a way to keep the hovercraft moving for a longer period of time by counteracting the effects of friction? Develop a plan to alter the hovercraft's design to reduce the amount of friction.

NAME ______________________ DATE ____________

NEWTON'S SECOND LAW

PHYSICAL SCIENCE

JUST THE FACTS

Newton's second law states that the amount of force on an object is equal to its mass multiplied by its acceleration. Scientists sometimes state this law in simpler terms by writing **F=ma.** (Force equals mass times acceleration.)

You can demonstrate this idea with a tennis ball and a kick ball. Take the balls outside to a large, open area. Throw the kick ball as hard as you can. Have a partner mark where it first hits the ground. Then, throw the tennis ball as hard as you can and have your partner mark where it hits the ground. What did you notice? What is the difference between the two balls? Can you come up with an explanation?

If you said that the kick ball has more mass than the tennis ball, you are correct! You attempted to use the same amount of force as you threw each ball, but in doing so, you gave the smaller ball more acceleration. This is essentially Newton's second law. For another fun demonstration of Newton's second law, try the following activity.

MATERIALS:

- 12" (30.48 cm) balloon
- 48" (121.92 cm) piece of yarn
- fishing line
- masking tape
- drinking straw
- 6 pennies
- meterstick
- paper cup
- small binder clip

PROCEDURE

1. Tape one end of the fishing line securely to the ceiling.
2. Thread the other end of the fishing line through a drinking straw. Then, tape the fishing line to a desk or another solid object. Be sure the straw can move freely on the fishing line.
3. Fully inflate the balloon and twist it closed. Attach a binder clip to the balloon to prevent it from deflating. To find the circumference of the fully inflated balloon, wrap yarn around the center of the balloon. Place your finger on the yarn to mark the distance around the balloon. Carefully transfer this length of yarn to the meterstick.

   The circumference of the balloon is ______________ cm.
4. Tape the balloon to the straw so that the balloon's opening faces downward toward the floor.
5. Remove the binder clip. The balloon should shoot toward the ceiling.
6. Discuss with your group members how you can make the balloon go higher on the fishing line by adding more force. Then, try it.
7. What do you think will happen if you add more mass? Inflate the balloon to the same circumference as in the first trial. Secure it with a binder clip. Tape a cup to the top of the balloon and place three pennies in the cup.
8. Release the balloon. Did it go as high as it did the first time? Why or why not?
9. Discuss with group members what will happen if you add three more pennies and use the same amount of force to launch the balloon. Then, try it.

NAME________________________________ DATE____________

NEWTON'S THIRD LAW

JUST THE FACTS

Newton's third law says that when you push an object, it pushes back with equal force but in the opposite direction. Newton stated it in more complicated terms, "For every action, there is an equal and opposite reaction."

To understand this better, you could grab a friend and head to the ice rink. Stand facing each other with your palms facing together and push against your friend. You should notice your friend moving away from you, but you should also notice that you are moving, as well. The distance you move will depend on your mass and the force with which you push. The following is another activity that demonstrates Newton's third law.

MATERIALS:

- white plastic film canister with snap-on lid
- antacid tablets
- water
- paper towels
- plastic knife
- beaker or graduated cylinder
- safety goggles

PROCEDURE

1. Put on the safety goggles. Use the beaker or graduated cylinder to add $1\frac{1}{2}$ tbsp (22 mL) of water to the film canister.
2. Add half of an antacid tablet and quickly snap the lid onto the canister. Your partner may need to hold the film canister for you as you do this step.
3. Place the canister lid-side down on the table.
4. Stand back and watch as the film canister launches into the air! If it does not launch, wait at least 30 seconds before examining the canister. Usually the cap is not on tight enough.
5. Clean the table with the paper towels. Then, try experimenting with different amounts of water, each time using half of an antacid tablet.

Based on your observations, describe how the launching film canister demonstrates Newton's third law of motion.

____

____

____

____

____

____

HIGHWAY CRASH CUSHIONS

SCIENCE IN SOCIETY

Cars and trucks travel at high speeds on highways. About one-third of highway injuries happen when vehicles hit solid objects, such as trees, poles, and street signs. Many injuries can be avoided if crash cushions are placed near these objects. When a vehicle hits a crash cushion, the cushion redirects the vehicle to a safe line of travel. The science behind crash cushions works the same way as the hovercraft and rocket models from the Newton's Laws of Motion experiments (pages 29–32). Engineers use different materials to create crash cushions. In this activity, you will determine how effective the materials are when used as crash cushions.

PHYSICAL SCIENCE

MATERIALS:

- 2-quart plastic container
- raw eggs
- 5' (1.52 m) length of 4" (10.16 cm) diameter PVC pipe
- permanent marker
- rubber bands (represents shredded rubber tires)
- plastic foam peanuts
- gravel
- aluminum foil (represents aluminum)
- sand
- small balloons (represents water barrels)
- water
- large, plastic tarp

PROCEDURE

1. Measure 2" (5.08 cm) from the top of the plastic container. Mark this height on the inside of the container with a permanent marker.
2. Spread the plastic tarp on the floor. Place the container on the tarp. Place masking tape on the tarp around the container to create a "footprint" of the container.
3. Move a chair near the container. Prop the PVC pipe on the back and seat edges of the chair, positioning the pipe so that the bottom opening of the pipe is over the plastic container.
4. Use a permanent marker to mark on the pipe where it touches the edges of the chair.
5. Place masking tape on the floor around the chair to create a "footprint" of the chair.
6. Drop the egg into the pipe. Watch carefully as the egg drops into the empty container. Write your observations of the egg's impact on another piece of paper.
7. Fill the plastic container to the line with plastic foam peanuts. Check the footprints and lines on the pipe to make sure the container, chair, and pipe have not moved. Reposition the items if necessary. Drop the egg into the pipe. Watch carefully as the egg drops into the container. How well did the material in the container absorb the impact of the egg? Did it redirect the egg after impact?
8. Repeat step 7 two additional times. Record the data on a data table.
9. Repeat steps 6–8 with the other materials (water balloons, sand, gravel, crumpled pieces of aluminum foil, and rubber bands).

TRY THIS! Based on your findings, explain which material you would recommend for engineers to use when building crash cushions.

NAME ______________________ DATE ____________

BALLOON-POWERED CARS

ENGINEERING CHALLENGE

CHALLENGE: Use the materials below to design and construct a car that can travel 7' (2.13 m) powered only by the air in a balloon.

GUIDELINES

- You must stay within a budget of $100, so plan your design carefully.
- Before you build the balloon-powered car, draw and label a picture of the car on another piece of paper.

Materials and Price List			Number of Materials		Cost of Materials
balloon	$20	x		=	
plastic foam tray	$10	x		=	
thumbtack	$5	x		=	
binder clip	$5	x		=	
drinking straw	$5	x		=	
washers	$5	x		=	
12" (30.48 cm) of tape	$10	x		=	
				Total Cost of Car:	

Conduct three trials of your balloon-powered car. Use a meterstick to measure the distance the balloon-powered car travels. Then, record the results on the data table and find the average distance traveled by the car.

DATA TABLE: Remember to label each measurement with the unit you used.

Trial 1	Trial 2	Trial 3	Average Distance

HOW MUCH AIR? SAMPLE EXPERIMENT

QUESTION: How does the amount of gas released from an object affect its movement?

HYPOTHESIS: If the amount of gas released from an object affects its movement, then the release of more gas will result in more movement of the object.

VARIABLES, CONTROL, AND CONSTANTS:

Independent variable: Amount of air blown into the balloon

Dependent variable: The distance the balloon-powered car travels

Control: A balloon-powered car with no air in the balloon

Constants: Variables that must remain the same

- type of balloon
- design of the balloon-powered car
- surface that the balloon-powered car travels on
- type of measuring tools
- method of measurement

MATERIALS:

- balloon-powered car (activity on page 34)
- 12" (30.48 cm) balloon
- meterstick
- small binder clip
- 20" (50.8 cm) of yarn
- masking tape
- permanent marker

PROCEDURE

1. Fully inflate the balloon and twist it closed. Attach a binder clip to the balloon to prevent it from deflating. To find the circumference of the fully-inflated balloon, wrap the yarn around the center of the balloon. Place your finger on the yarn to mark the distance around the balloon. Carefully transfer this length of yarn to the meterstick.

   Divide this measurement into fourths. Record these lengths on a data table. Wrap small pieces of masking tape at each of these lengths on the yarn. Use a permanent marker to label each measurement on the masking tape. (These measurements will serve as the independent variables.)

   For example, if a fully inflated balloon has a circumference of 12" (30.48 cm), then one-fourth of the circumference is 3" (7.65 cm). This length of yarn can be wrapped around the circumference of a balloon that is one-fourth inflated.
2. Place an 8" (20.32 cm) piece of masking tape on the floor to mark the starting point.
3. Secure the balloon to the balloon-powered car. Using the labeled yarn to measure, fill the balloon until it is one-fourth inflated. Twist the balloon so that the air does not escape.
4. Place the car on the floor at the starting point and untwist the balloon. When the car comes to a complete stop, use a meterstick to measure the distance in centimeters that the balloon-powered car traveled.
5. Record the distance on the data table and repeat steps 3–4 two more times. Find the average distance traveled and record it on the data table.
6. Repeat steps 3–5 for each amount of air (one-half, three-fourths, and fully inflated).

NAME________________________ DATE__________

HOW MUCH AIR?

EXPERIMENTAL DESIGN

Engineers are constantly looking for ways to improve their designs. Sometimes this involves changing different **variables** to determine which improvements to make.

TASK: Design an experiment to determine the how changing the amount of air affects the distance that a balloon-powered car travels. Complete the worksheets (pages 10–14) as you design and perform your How Much Air? experiment.

HINTS

HYPOTHESIS:

- Think about what you already know about balloon-powered cars based on the Balloon-Powered Cars experiment (page 34).

VARIABLES, CONTROL, AND CONSTANTS:

- What will you test?
- What will change as a result of the independent variable?
- To which trial will you compare all of the results?
- Which parts of the experiment must stay the same?

GRAPH:

- Create a graph that shows a picture of the data you collected in this experiment. Remember to label both axes and give the graph an appropriate title.

NAME ______________________ DATE ______________

NEWTON'S BALLOON CARS

THE "WRITE" STUFF

Now that you have completed several activities to learn about Newton's laws of motion, on the lines below, state Newton's three laws of motion in your own words. Use examples from your experiments to describe how each law relates to the movement of a balloon-powered car.

PHYSICAL SCIENCE

NAME______________________________ DATE______________

FORCE AND MOTION CROSSWORD

JUST THE FACTS

Use the vocabulary terms from the word bank below to complete the crossword puzzle.

WORD BANK					
mass	second	inertia	Newton	force	acceleration
first	third	friction	propulsion	momentum	motion

ACROSS

1. the amount of matter in an object
3. name of the man who developed the three laws of motion
4. Newton's ______________ law states, "For every action, there is an equal and opposite reaction."
6. motion that drives forward or onward
7. the push two objects give when they rub against each other
8. tendency of an object to continue doing what it is already doing, dependent upon the object's mass
9. a change in an object's motion (This term is often confused with speed.)

DOWN

1. movement
2. Newton's ______________ law states F=ma.
5. Newton's ______________ law states, "An object in motion will say in motion unless something else causes it to stop or change direction."
7. any action between two objects that changes their motion or state of rest

NAME______________________________________DATE____________________

MEET TODD BARBER

SPOTLIGHT ON SCIENTISTS

Todd Barber is an **aerospace engineer** who works at the Jet Propulsion Laboratory in Pasadena, California. He designs rocket engines for robotic missions to other planets. His job is to test the rockets to make sure they work properly and provide enough propulsion to launch the spacecrafts into space. **Propulsion** is the force that drives an object forward. One part of Mr. Barber's job involves thinking about things that might go wrong with the rockets in space. He needs to figure out how to solve these problems before the rocket is launched because it is not easy to repair the spacecraft once it leaves Earth.

Mr. Barber became interested in spacecraft as a child when he read about the *Voyager* missions to the outer solar system. To learn about working with robotic spacecrafts, he attended college at the Massachusetts Institute of Technology, one of the best engineering schools in the United States. He has been part of many successful robotic missions, including the *Galileo* spacecraft mission to Jupiter, the *Cassini* mission to Saturn, and the Mars Exploration Rover mission.

Choose one of the robotic missions that Mr. Barber helped to launch. Use science books, encyclopedias, or the Internet to research the required information. Write your answers on the lines below. If you need more space, continue your answers on another piece of paper.

REQUIRED INFORMATION

- What is the goal of the mission?
- When did the robotic spacecraft leave Earth?
- How long did it take for the spacecraft to reach its destination?
- What has the robotic spacecraft helped scientists learn about the planet?
- When is/was the scheduled end of the mission?

Robotic Mission: ____

NAME________________________________ DATE______________

THE METRIC SYSTEM

SCIENCE SKILLS

PHYSICAL SCIENCE

Most countries use the **metric system** of measurement (meters, liters, grams, etc.). The metric system is based on multiples of 10, which makes it easy to convert measurements to different units. Scientists around the world use the metric system as a standard form of communication. It is important to understand this system of measurement, especially if you will be conducting science experiments. Use the following metric chart to help you convert the metric measurements below.

Length	Mass	Volume
10 mm = 1 cm	1,000 mg = 1 g	1,000 mL = 1 L
100 cm = 1 m	1,000 g = 1 kg	
1,000 m = 1 km		

1. 23 cm = ______________ mm
2. 100 cm = ______________ m
3. 35.4 mm = ______________ cm
4. 0.5 km = ______________ m
5. 5,000 m = ______________ km
6. 678.3 g = ______________ kg
7. 34.26 mg = ______________ g
8. 0.067 kg = ______________ g
9. 1 L = ______________ mL
10. 12.4 g = ______________ kg
11. 0.002 kg = ______________ g
12. 1,000 mL = ______________ L
13. 10 mL = ______________ L
14. 5.62 g = ______________ mg
15. 236. 2 mL = ______________ L
16. 0.0036 L = ______________ mL
17. 4,581 mL = ______________ L
18. 0.025 kg = ______________ g

NAME ______________________ DATE __________

CONDUCTORS AND INSULATORS

ENGINEERING CHALLENGE

A **conductor** is a type of material or object that allows heat, electricity, or sound to flow easily through it. An **insulator** is a type of material or object that restricts the flow of heat, electricity, or sound. A **circuit** is circular route that provides a path for electricity to flow. A closed electrical circuit allows electricity to flow uninterrupted through each object in the circuit. When a circuit is open in one location, the flow of electricity stops.

CHALLENGE: Using the materials below, create a closed electrical circuit that will light a lightbulb. Then, test the objects listed at the bottom of this page in the circuit to determine if they are conductors or insulators of electricity.

MATERIALS:

- 6-volt lantern battery
- flashlight bulb
- objects from conductors and insulators list
- 3 pieces of insulated copper wire
- electrical tape

GUIDELINES

- To create a closed electrical circuit that will light a lightbulb, the wires, a battery, and a lightbulb must be included in the circuit.
- After you have successfully created a closed circuit, decide how you will test each object listed below to determine if it is a conductor or an insulator of electricity. Try the paper clip first. If the lightbulb lights with the paper clip in the circuit, you have successfully created a testing device for conductors and insulators.
- Draw a closed electrical circuit and a closed circuit with one test object on the data table on page 42.

Predict whether the following objects are **conductors** or **insulators**. Write *C* for conductor or *I* for insulator.

a) paper clip ______

b) string ______

c) steel nail ______

d) plastic ruler ______

e) piece of cotton fabric ______

f) tab from a soft drink can ______

g) crayon ______

h) potato ______

i) rubber band ______

j) paper ______

k) ______ (your choice) ______

l) ______ (your choice) ______

NAME______________________________DATE______________

PHYSICAL SCIENCE

DATA TABLE:

Closed Electrical Circuit	Closed Electrical Circuit with Test Object

Use your device to test the objects listed on page 41. On the lines below, record whether each object is a **conductor** or an **insulator**. Write *C* for conductor or *I* for insulator.

a) paper clip ______________

b) string ______________

c) steel nail ______________

d) plastic ruler ______________

e) piece of cotton fabric ______________

f) tab from a soft drink can ______________

g) crayon ______________

h) potato ______________

i) rubber band ______________

j) paper ______________

k) ______________ ______________
(your choice)

l) ______________ ______________
(your choice)

On another piece of paper, answer the following questions in complete sentences.

1. Describe how you were able to determine whether each object you tested was a **conductor** or an **insulator**.
2. Of the objects that you classified as conductors, name several physical characteristics that they have in common.
3. Of the objects that you classified as insulators, name several physical characteristics that they have in common.

FAST-FOOD FRENZY SAMPLE EXPERIMENT

QUESTION: How is the amount of heat an object retains affected by the type of material used to insulate it?

HYPOTHESIS: If the type of insulating materials affects the amount of heat an object retains, then an object insulated with plastic foam will retain the most heat.

VARIABLES, CONTROL, AND CONSTANTS:

Independent variable: Type of material used for insulation

Dependent variable: Amount of heat retained by the insulated object in a set amount of time

Control: An object that is uninsulated

Constants: Variables that must remain the same

- type of object to be insulated
- method of insulation placement
- temperature and amount of heated water
- type of measuring tools
- method of measurement
- type of container for hot water

MATERIALS:

- plastic foam peanuts
- cardboard strips
- 2 scientific thermometers
- shoe box with lid
- empty metal can
- aluminum foil
- hot glue gun
- pen or pencil
- hot water

PROCEDURE

1. With a pen or pencil, carefully poke two small holes in the lid of the shoe box—one near the center of the lid and one in a corner of the lid.
2. Choose one type of insulating material (plastic foam peanuts, cardboard strips, or aluminum foil). Use the hot glue gun to attach the insulation to the inside walls and lid of the shoe box. Do not cover the holes in the lid of the shoe box.
3. Glue the same type of insulation around the metal can.
4. Place the metal can in the same corner of the box as the hole in the lid. After your teacher pours hot water into the can, place the lid on the box.
5. Carefully insert the thermometers into the holes in the lid. One thermometer will measure the temperature of the water inside the can. The other will measure the air temperature inside the shoe box.
6. Record the starting temperature of the water in the can and the air temperature of the shoe box on the data table.
7. Record the water and air temperatures in the shoe box every five minutes for one hour.
8. Compare the final results for your type of insulation with the other types used by your classmates and with a shoe box that has no insulation.

PHYSICAL SCIENCE

NAME______________________ DATE__________

FAST-FOOD FRENZY

EXPERIMENTAL DESIGN

Do you notice different types of packaging that fast food is served in? Restaurants often use containers made from plastic foam, cardboard, or aluminum foil to keep food warm for longer periods of time. These materials are called insulators. An **insulator** is a type of material or object that restricts the flow of heat, electricity, or sound.

TASK: Design an experiment to determine which type of insulating material used in fast-food containers retains heat for the longest amount of time. Complete the worksheets (pages 10–14) as you design and perform your Fast-Food Frenzy experiment.

HINTS

HYPOTHESIS:

- Think about what you already know about the types of materials from which fast-food containers are made. You may wish to research how the materials are created and how they work as insulators.

VARIABLES, CONTROL, AND CONSTANTS:

- What will you test?
- What will change as a result of the independent variable?
- To which trial will you compare all of the results?
- Which parts of the experiment must stay the same?

GRAPH:

- Create a graph that shows a picture of the data you collected in this experiment. Remember to label both axes and give the graph an appropriate title.

NUCLEAR POWER

THE "WRITE" STUFF

The two people pictured below have opposing opinions about the use of nuclear energy and radiation. Read each viewpoint. Then, use science books, magazines, or the Internet to research nuclear energy to help you decide what you think about its use. On another piece of paper, write a persuasive letter to your local newspaper to state your opinion about the use of nuclear energy, as well as address the opposing viewpoint.

OPINION #1:

"The use of radioactive material is extremely beneficial to our society. Nuclear power is clean burning and provides a lot of energy for little cost. If you have ever had an X-ray, eaten certain types of pork or poultry, known anyone who has been treated for cancer with radiation therapy, or wondered how scientists determine the age of fossils, then you are probably aware of the benefits of radiation.

X-rays use radiation to view the bones inside the body. This invention has revolutionized the way doctors practice medicine by allowing them to identify internal problems immediately. Many types of meat, poultry, fruit, and vegetables are irradiated by passing a small amount of radiation through the food to kill bacteria and other microorganisms. Radiation therapy is often used to detect and treat certain types of cancers. Finally, radioisotopic dating allows scientists to determine the age of dinosaur bones and other fossils so that we can learn more about the history of life on our planet.

In closing, the advantages of nuclear energy and radiation heavily outweigh the risks. We should develop more uses for nuclear energy so that society will continue to benefit."

OPINION #2:

"The use of nuclear energy is extremely dangerous to people all over the world. Thousands of people died in Japan when the United States used atomic bombs during World War II. Other countries are now trying to develop their own nuclear weapons that could be used against their enemies.

Many people think that nuclear power is safer than other kinds of power. However, nuclear power plants produce waste products that take thousands of years to break down. Finding a place to store this waste is a huge problem. Transporting the waste to distant locations for disposal is also difficult. Would you want a nuclear waste disposal facility near your home?

In addition, even though the risk of a core meltdown is small, it has happened in the past. In 1986, a fire at the nuclear facility in Chernobyl in the Soviet Union resulted in a meltdown of its core reactor. The wind carried radiation, and thousands of people throughout the Ukraine died from exposure to radiation. No one should be endangered by a similar tragedy.

We need to investigate and perfect alternative forms of energy, such as coal, oil, hydroelectric, geothermal, wind, and solar power. Our world would be much safer if nuclear research, power, and weapons were banned."

RENEWABLE ENERGY SOURCES

SCIENCE IN SOCIETY

One of the biggest issues in our society is finding **renewable energy sources**. Renewable energy, such as hydroelectric, solar, wind, geothermal, and the use of biomass, creates electricity from natural resources that can be replaced or "renewed." Although no energy production is perfect, these renewable energy sources cause less harm to the environment than other energy sources. They also contribute less to global warming and the greenhouse effect than fossil fuels, such as coal and oil.

Use science books, magazines, or the Internet to research one of these renewable energy sources. Create a poster to present to your class that includes the required information below.

REQUIRED INFORMATION

- Description of the renewable energy source and how it is created
- Cost of the energy source compared to other energy sources
- Effect of the energy source on the environment
- Ability of the energy source to provide the amount of energy required by our society
- Advantages and disadvantages of using the energy source
- Pictures or drawings of the energy source and how it is created

DOWNHILL FUN

SCIENCE SKILLS

When you are sledding, have you ever wondered why your sled moves faster on some hills than others? Why do some people on sleds get to the bottom of the hill before others? The answer lies in the energy used between the top and bottom of the hill. In this activity, you will use your science skills of **measuring** and **timing** while you learn about potential and kinetic energy. **Potential energy** is energy stored in an object. **Kinetic energy** is the energy of a moving object.

MATERIALS:

- wax paper
- salt
- water
- butter
- flour
- large piece of cardboard
- masking tape
- chair or large books
- checkers
- stopwatch
- permanent marker
- paper towels
- ruler
- scissors

PROCEDURE

1. To create your slopes, cut a piece of cardboard into strips 6" (15.24 cm) wide x 3' (91 cm) long. Cut a sheet of wax paper into five strips 4" (10.16 cm) wide x 3' (91 cm) long.
2. Place a strip of wax paper on each slope and tape it to the cardboard at the top and bottom.

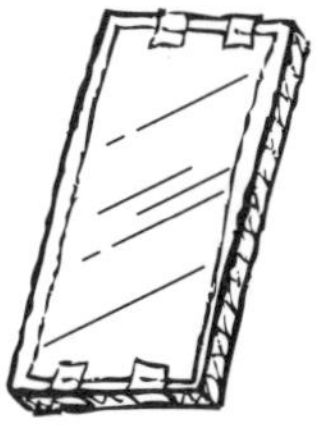

3. Label the slopes 1–5 with a permanent marker.
4. Change a variable of the wax paper surface of each slope as follows:
   Slope 1: Drizzle some water and sprinkle salt on the surface.
   Slope 2: Use a paper towel to spread a thin layer of butter on the surface.
   Slope 3: Sprinkle a layer of flour on the surface.
   Slope 4: Crumple the waxed paper into a ball and smooth it out. You may have to retape it to the cardboard.
   Slope 5: Do not do anything to the wax paper. This slope is the **control**.
5. Prop each cardboard slope on the large books or a chair at a 45° angle. Make sure all of the slopes have exactly the same angle.
6. Place a checker at the top of first slope and release it. Use the stopwatch to time how long it takes for the checker to reach the bottom of the slope or to stop moving. Record the time on the data table. Then, measure and record the distance it traveled down the slope. Repeat for slopes 2–5.

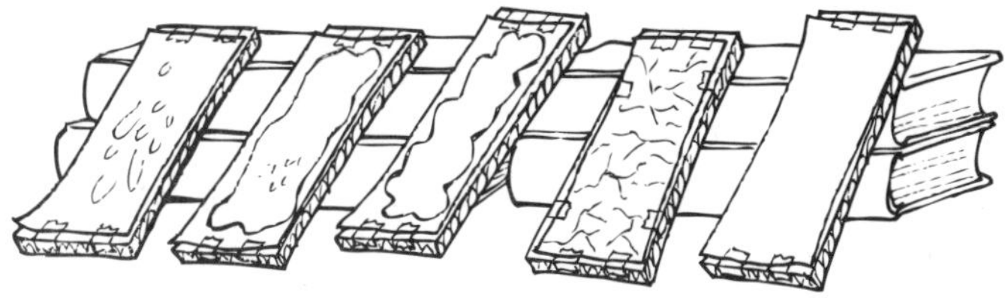

PHYSICAL SCIENCE

NAME________________________________ DATE______________

DATA TABLE: Remember to label each measurement with the unit you used.

Downhill Slope	Distance Traveled	Time
Slope 1		
Slope 2		
Slope 3		
Slope 4		
Slope 5		

RESULTS: Answer the following questions in complete sentences.

1. A checker at the top of a slope is an example of ______________________ energy. Explain your answer. (potential/kinetic)

____

____

2. A checker moving down a slope is an example of ______________________ energy. Explain your answer. (potential/kinetic)

____

____

3. On which slope did the checker have the most kinetic energy? How do you know?

____

____

____

4. On which slope did the checker have the least kinetic energy? How do you know?

____

____

____

TRY THIS! Use the data from this activity to create a bar graph comparing the distance traveled on the five different types of slopes.

NAME____________________DATE__________

MORE DOWNHILL FUN

SCIENCE SKILLS

Now that you have had some experience with changing variables on downhill slopes, it is time to develop some of your own ideas! In this activity, you will build upon the knowledge that you learned in Downhill Fun (page 47) by making **predictions** about how increasing the mass and air resistance will affect the speed of the sled as it moves down a slope.

MATERIALS:

- wax paper
- salt
- water
- butter
- flour
- large piece of cardboard
- checkers
- 2 quarters
- masking tape
- chair or large books
- stopwatch
- permanent marker
- paper towels
- ruler
- scissors
- electric fan

1. Predict how the speed of the checker will change if you conduct the slope experiments with two quarters taped to the top.

____

____

____

2. Predict how the speed of the checker will change if you conduct the slope experiments with a fan placed at the bottom of the slope to blow air toward the checker as it moves.

____

____

____

PROCEDURE

1. Follow steps 1–5 from Downhill Fun (page 47) to create the five different downhill slopes.
2. Tape two quarters to the top of a checker. Conduct the slope experiments using this altered checker. Record the results on Data Table 1 on page 50. Remove the quarters from the checker.
3. Place the electric fan at the bottom of Slope 1. Angle the fan so that it blows air up the slope. Turn the fan on medium speed and conduct the first slope experiment. Record the results on Data Table 2 on page 50. Repeat for the remaining slopes.
4. Try using different slope angles or different slope materials. On another piece of paper, write a materials list and a numbered procedure. Create a data table to display the data. Conduct the experiments and share your results with the class!

PHYSICAL SCIENCE

NAME____DATE____________________

DATA TABLE 1: Remember to label each measurement with the unit you used.

Checker with Two Quarters Taped to the Top		
Downhill Slope	**Distance Traveled**	**Time**
Slope 1		
Slope 2		
Slope 3		
Slope 4		
Slope 5		

DATA TABLE 2: Remember to label each measurement with the unit you used.

Electric Fan Blowing Air up the Slope		
Downhill Slope	**Distance Traveled**	**Time**
Slope 1		
Slope 2		
Slope 3		
Slope 4		
Slope 5		

RESULTS: Answer the following questions in complete sentences.

1. What did you discover about the addition of mass and its relationship to kinetic and potential energy?

____

____

____

2. How is using the electric fan like a model of downhill sledding in real life? How does using a fan affect the checker's kinetic energy?

____

____

____

NAME____________________________DATE____________

TYPES OF ENERGY

JUST THE FACTS

Fill in the blank with a word from the word bank to correctly complete each sentence. Use a dictionary, science book, or the Internet to complete this activity.

WORD BANK					
radiant	thermal	chemical	mechanical	electrical	nuclear

1. ______________________ energy is contained in things that are moving or about to move. When it is stored, it is also called **potential energy**. When it is in motion, it is also called **kinetic energy.**

2. ______________________ energy is usually called light energy, but TV and radio waves are also common examples. Sunlight is often a source of this energy.

3. ______________________ energy is caused by the movement of electrons. It is often used to operate appliances, such as a dishwasher, toaster, or blender. This energy comes from things like batteries or generators.

4. ______________________ energy is also known as heat energy. It works by causing the molecules of a substance to move faster, which creates the heat. If you want to create some of your own type of this energy, try rubbing your hands together. This causes **friction**, another form of this energy.

5. ______________________ energy is locked in the nucleus of an atom. It can be produced by splitting the atom in a process called **fission** or by fusing two atoms together in a process called **fusion**. Fusion takes place in the sun.

6. ______________________ energy is released when chemical bonds are broken. It is contained in food, wood, and petroleum fuels. We produce this kind of energy by digesting food or burning fossil fuels.

Label each activity with its correct type of energy from the word bank.

7. Digesting a cheeseburger______________________
8. Boiling water______________________
9. Using a battery to play a radio ______________________
10. Gears turning the wheels on a bicycle ______________________
11. Solar power cells providing electricity to a home ______________________
12. Reactions taking place in stars ______________________

PHYSICAL SCIENCE

MEET DR. AYANNA HOWARD

SPOTLIGHT ON SCIENTISTS

Dr. Ayanna Howard's all-time favorite television show is *The Bionic Woman*, so it is no wonder she chose to dedicate her life to the study of robotics! Dr. Howard became interested in robotics during high school when she discovered her love for mathematics. This led her to study **electrical engineering** in college.

Dr. Howard works at the Jet Propulsion Laboratory in Pasadena, California. This division of NASA is responsible for robotic missions to other planets. Dr. Howard's job is to develop intelligent robots that can make decisions without directions from humans. One of her current projects involves developing software that allows a robot to look at an area's landscape and choose a place to land. This is a lot more complicated than it sounds! For example, say while you are walking, you see a toy truck in the middle of the sidewalk. To avoid tripping over the toy, first you must notice it; decide to avoid it; make the decision to move left, right, or over the top of it; and finally walk around or over it. Keep in mind that you have probably done all of these things while having a conversation with your friend, carrying a backpack, and not missing a step.

While this doesn't seem like a complicated series of actions, it would be very difficult for a robot to do! This is why engineers like Dr. Howard have a tough job. They need to consider many different factors and movements each time they program a robot to do a certain task. If you want to learn more about these and other missions, you can explore the Jet Propulsion Laboratory Web site: www.jpl.nasa.gov.

Most robots need instructions from a programmer in order to complete a job. The instructions must be complete and detailed since the robot will do exactly what its programming instructions tell it to do. For this activity, you will need the help of your classmates.

GUIDELINES

1. Choose one student to be the "robot."
2. Blindfold the robot so that she cannot see anything.
3. Choose a task for the robot to complete. This could be picking up an object across the room, sharpening a pencil, walking through an obstacle course of desks, etc.
4. Everyone else in the room is a "programmer." Take turns giving a one-sentence instruction to the robot. Each person is allowed to give only one instruction at a time! Continue instructions until the task is complete.

DISCUSSION: Discuss the following questions with your classmates.

1. What was the most difficult part of "programming" your "robot"?
2. What was the easiest part of programming your robot?
3. Why is it important to give precise directions to a robot?

EARTH SCIENCE TEACHER TIPS

Using Models (page 55)

Nectarines are available in most grocery stores in the summer and fall seasons. Plastic knives used by students should be able to cut through a nectarine. This activity will also work well as a demonstration.

Candy Bar Core Samples (page 56)

Choose candy bars that have multiple layers of different ingredients. For example, candy bars that have several layers of chocolate, peanut butter, nougat, or caramel all make interesting choices.

Caution: Before completing any food activity, ask families' permission and inquire about students' food allergies and religious or other food preferences.

Gold Rush! (page 59)

A large, aluminum baking tray (available at most grocery stores) will work well for the large tub required for each group. Before class, create the soil mixture by mixing about 200 BBs in a bucket of sandy soil.

Boat Building (page 60)

Allow students to experiment with different boat designs to find the one that will support the greatest mass. An example of a successful design is a square or rectangular-shaped boat with a flat bottom and raised edges. This design provides a large bottom surface area to help the boat stay afloat.

Meet Brian Fisher (page 63)

Divide students into groups of three or four. Explain that they will be investigating the way a plume travels through underground aquifers by performing a plume simulation. A plume is a continuous emission of contamination that has a beginning point and a noticeable path. Contamination plumes can spread thousands of feet from where the source began, and may remain in the soil after the contamination is cleaned up.

Digging for the Past (page 65)

Plastic bones may be purchased at a Halloween, novelty, or pet store. Choose a variety of "artifacts" (pencils, paper clips, bottle caps, eating utensils) for students to use for this activity.

Problem Solving (page 66)

Problem solving is an important skill for students to practice, especially since conducting an experiment requires that students attempt to find the answer to a problem. This activity will model problem solving similar to what might be experienced by scientists working on a fossil dig.

Before class, find at least 10 pictures of various animals. Pictures can be found in magazines or printed from the Internet on a color printer.

Cut each color picture into puzzle pieces. Depending on the age and experience level of students, you can make the activity more difficult by cutting the pieces smaller. Place the pieces of each puzzle into a manila envelope.

Divide the class into pairs. Give each pair of students an envelope and instruct them to follow the procedure on page 66.

To create an extra challenge for students, mix the pieces of two puzzles together. This simulates finding the fossilized remains of more than one animal in a location.

If Fossils Could Talk! (page 67)

The picture of the bird footprint fossil is different from the other three fossils pictured on this page. Sometimes fossilized remains do not come in the form of bones. Fossilized footprints are called **trace fossils**.

Hurricane House (page 68)

Divide students into groups of three or four. Students can use the materials provided to construct a house that will withstand a storm surge and winds of a simulated hurricane. They should create a beach using sand. Sand, twigs, and rocks can be used to build a sea wall or jetty to protect their model house.

An example of a basic miniature house can be created using craft sticks, duct tape, small rocks, and plastic interlocking blocks.

1. Construct the frame of the house by creating a cube structure with craft sticks and duct tape.
2. Bury the bottom portion of the cube in the sand of the model beach. Anchor it to the beach by placing small rocks around the perimeter of the structure.

Hurricane House (continued)

3. Create the walls of the house with plastic interlocking blocks. Place these walls between the vertical craft sticks of the house's frame.
4. Use craft sticks and duct tape to create a roof for the house.
5. The house may be fortified by creating a sea wall with additional small rocks, sand, and sticks.

Note: Although some structures will withstand repeated waves from the storm surge and wind, the model beach that students create will eventually be eroded by the forces of water and wind, making the house structure unstable. This can lead to discussions about the cost and impact on communities from the natural erosion of coastal areas.

Meet Dr. Gretchen Jones (page 72)

Prior to conducting this activity, you can create an outline map of the classroom to distribute. Inform the administrators and custodians that during this simulation, "pollen" dots will be spread throughout the school. During the mapping portion of this activity, you may wish to have students pick up the "pollen" dots after they have marked the locations on their maps.

Mission Measurement (page 73)

This lesson will provide students with additional practice of performing metric unit conversions. Students should have a basic understanding of the conversions between kilometers, meters, centimeters, and millimeters before completing this activity.

Mission Measurement (continued)

Provide each student with an instructional card (page 74). Then, group students so that each group has at least one student with each type of card. The object students build is a parachute with a paper cup basket.

Martian Landing Gear (page 77)

Caution: Raw eggs may be contaminated with salmonella, a bacteria responsible for food poisoning. To prevent illness from bacteria, use only properly refrigerated, clean, unbroken, fresh, grade AA or A eggs. Have students wash hands thoroughly after completing this activity. Or consider using pasteurized eggs, which have been treated to destroy the salmonella bacteria.

An example of a simple egg landing device can be created by following this procedure.

1. Carefully wrap an egg in a paper towel.
2. Press several paper towels into two plastic foam cups, leaving room for the egg. Do not pack the paper towels too tightly. If a small amount of space is left inside of the cup to absorb the shock of the fall, the egg should not break.
3. Carefully place the egg into one of the cups.
4. Tape the openings of the cups together.

Encourage students to use additional teacher-approved materials to construct their egg landing devices. When dropping the egg landing devices from higher locations, consider using the top of an open staircase or the gym bleachers.

Moon Phases (page 79)

After a period of about 28 days, each student should have a complete moon phase chart. This activity should be conducted over a period of several months, as some days or nights may be overcast and the moon may not be visible. Also, when a scientist performs an experiment, she conducts many trials to ensure the accuracy of her results. Each month of this experiment can be considered one trial, and therefore, should be repeated.

USING MODELS

SCIENCE SKILLS

From a human perspective, Earth is a very large place. We live on a very small part of what makes up the entire planet. To explain ideas that might be too difficult or too large to demonstrate in real life, such as visualizing the size of Earth, scientists use **models**. In this activity, you will use a nectarine to model how the inside of Earth looks and represents areas on Earth's surface.

MATERIALS:

- nectarine
- plastic knife
- paper towels
- pencil

PROCEDURE

1. Draw a light line around the center of the nectarine to represent the **equator**. Carefully cut the nectarine in half on the line. This should create two equal halves of the fruit. Examine the inside of the fruit. What you see is a model of the inside of Earth.
2. Observe the thickness of the skin. If Earth were the size of the nectarine, this skin would be the thickness of Earth's **crust**.
3. The fleshy part of the fruit would be Earth's **mantle**. The mantle is made of melted rock called **magma**. If there is a break in the crust, magma can rise to the surface and may eventually create a volcano!
4. Examine the pit of the nectarine. This represents Earth's **outer core**, which is made of liquid iron and nickel.
5. Inside the pit is a seed. This represents Earth's **inner core**, which is solid iron and nickel. The metals in the core produce Earth's magnetic field.
6. Think about the part of Earth on which humans can live. Since oceans cover three-fourths of Earth's surface, cut the top half of the nectarine in half. The piece you have left is one-fourth of the whole nectarine. The skin of this quarter represents the total amount of land area on Earth.
7. Many mountains are unsuitable for humans to live on due to cold temperatures and high altitudes. Mountains cover one-third of the land area on Earth. Cut off one-third of the piece you have left.
8. Deserts and glaciers are often unsuitable for humans due to extreme temperature and little usable water. Deserts and glaciers cover another one-third of Earth's land area. Cut off one-half of the piece you have left.
9. The skin on the remaining section of the nectarine represents the total land area where people and land plants and animals must live.

TRY THIS! On another piece of paper, draw a picture of how the inside of Earth looks based on your observations of the nectarine model. Label the crust, mantle, and inner and outer cores.

NAME______________________________DATE__________________

CANDY BAR CORE SAMPLES

SCIENCE SKILLS

It is not always practical for scientists to dig a large hole to see what is beneath Earth's surface. Instead, they use a method called **core sampling**. To take a core sample, scientists drill into Earth's crust and bring up a long, cylindrical sample of the rock underneath. This allows scientists to view the rock layers without the time-consuming process of digging large holes. You can use a **model** to visualize how scientists use core samples to view deep layers of rock.

MATERIALS:

- 3 different types of candy bars
- colorful pencils or markers
- 3 large, clear, drinking straws

PROCEDURE

1. Unwrap the three candy bars. Write several detailed observations about each candy bar surface (texture, color, shape, etc.) in the data table below.
2. To create your core sample, carefully push a straw through the first candy bar until it comes out the other side. You may need to twist the straw as you push it through the candy bar.
3. Remove the straw from the candy bar and examine the sample. This is a good representation of what the inside of the candy bar looks like. Draw a picture of each core sample in the data table below.

DATA TABLE:

Name of Candy Bar	Observations of Candy Bar Surface	Drawing of Core Sample

EARTH SCIENCE

NAME________________________ DATE____________

ROCKS AND MINERALS

JUST THE FACTS

Label the following rocks and minerals as either a **mineral** or an **igneous**, **sedimentary**, or **metamorphic rock**. Use a dictionary, science book, or the Internet to complete this activity.

1. gneiss ____________
2. halite ____________
3. limestone ____________
4. granite ____________
5. conglomerate ____________
6. obsidian ____________
7. mica ____________
8. sulfur ____________
9. schist ____________
10. shale ____________
11. marble ____________
12. sandstone ____________
13. basalt ____________
14. pumice ____________
15. quartz ____________
16. slate ____________
17. hematite ____________
18. magnetite ____________
19. hornblende ____________
20. calcite ____________

EARTH SCIENCE

NAME_______________________________________DATE_____________

TRIP TO THE CENTER OF EARTH

THE "WRITE" STUFF

Write a narrative story about taking a trip to the center of Earth, describing your experiences as you pass through each layer. You may choose to write a surprise ending about what you see once you reach Earth's core. Use descriptive words to help the reader feel what it would be like to go along on this journey.

EARTH SCIENCE

GOLD RUSH!

SCIENCE IN SOCIETY

During the 1800s, many prospectors, had dreams of finding a fortune in gold and made the long journey to California in hopes of striking it rich. They used a process called **sluicing** to separate the gold from other rocks and minerals that were commonly found in streams and rivers. Although modern technology has created better and faster ways to prospect for gold, people still use sluicing today. In this activity, you will model this process as you prospect for "gold."

MATERIALS:

- soil mixture (prepared by the teacher)
- customary unit balance
- pie tin
- water
- plastic cup
- large tub
- small hand shovel

PROCEDURE

1. Use the shovel to place two scoops of soil mixture into the pie tin.
2. Fill the plastic cup with water. Hold the pie tin directly over the large, empty tub. Have your partner slowly pour the water over the pie tin while you swirl the soil over the large, empty tub. This is called sluicing. The soil will swirl out of the pie tin, but the heavier gold will stay on the bottom. After all of the of soil is removed, you should have some BBs, which represent "gold" pieces left in your pie tin.
3. Weigh the gold pieces in ounces. (Prospectors measured gold in the customary unit of ounces.) Record the weight of the gold on the data table below.
4. Repeat steps 1–3 two more times. Then, find the total weight of your gold.

DATA TABLE: Remember to label each measurement with the unit you used.

Trial 1	Trial 2	Trial 3	Total Weight

On another piece of paper, answer the following questions in complete sentences.

1. Did your sluicing technique improve after the first trial? Why or why not?
2. Why did you uncover larger amounts of gold in some trials and smaller amounts in others?
3. Do you think panning for gold is more a measure of skill or a measure of luck? Explain your answer.
4. The price of gold is always changing. Use the Internet to find the current price of one ounce of gold. How much money would you have if someone paid you for the "gold" you found today?
5. In reality, you probably discovered more gold during this activity than a prospector would find in a week! Knowing this, do you think you would leave your home in search of a fortune? Why or why not?

NAME____________________ DATE__________

BOAT BUILDING

ENGINEERING CHALLENGE

Water is an important natural resource. It covers three-fourths of Earth's surface, and plants, animals, and people all depend on it for survival. People use water for many different purposes, such as growing crops, drinking, and cleaning. People have also found a way to use waterways and oceans as a means of transportation. Oceans and rivers are an important way of transporting goods and natural resources, such as oil, clothing, and food.

CHALLENGE: Design a boat that can hold the most weight.

MATERIALS:

- 3" x 3" (7.62 cm x 7.62 cm) square of aluminum foil
- 4 craft sticks
- 12" (30.48 cm) piece of masking tape
- metric balance
- large tub of water
- weights (pennies or paper clips)
- small ball of clay

PROCEDURE

1. Brainstorm ideas for the boat's design with your group. Decide on one design and construct the boat using the materials listed above.
2. Carefully place the boat into the tub of water.
3. One at a time, place weights into the boat. When you notice the first drops of water entering the boat, stop adding weights. Count the number of weights in the boat and place them on the balance. Record the mass of the weights on the data table below.
4. Repeat steps 2 and 3 two more times. Then, calculate the average mass your boat could hold.
5. Make adjustments to the design of the boat so that it will hold more weight. Then, repeat the experiment. Compare your boats' designs and results with your classmates' results to find which group's boat held the most weight.

DATA TABLE: Remember to label each measurement with the unit you used.

Boat	Trial 1	Trial 2	Trial 3	Average Mass
Design 1				
Design 2				

EARTH SCIENCE

TALKING TRASH SAMPLE EXPERIMENT

QUESTION: How does the amount of exposure to the natural elements of wind, precipitation, and heat from the sun affect an object's rate of decomposition?

HYPOTHESIS: If the amount of exposure to the natural elements affects an object's rate of decomposition, then an object that is fully exposed to the natural elements will decompose in the least amount of time.

VARIABLES, CONTROL, AND CONSTANTS:

Independent variable: Amount of exposure to the natural elements

Dependent variable: Rate of decomposition of objects (based on a student-created observation scale)

Control: A sample of objects that is not exposed to the natural elements

Constants: Variables that must remain the same

- type of objects
- approximate mass of objects
- amount of time between observations
- measurement tools and scale
- method of measurement
- location of testing area

MATERIALS:

- 3 banana peels
- 3 apple cores
- 3 soft drink bottles (16 oz.)
- 3 paper napkins
- shoe box
- clear, plastic trash bag
- clear, plastic container
- electric drill

PROCEDURE

1. Designate an outdoor area where the garbage can be placed without being disturbed. This area should receive full exposure to the natural elements.
2. Place one of each type of garbage in the clear, plastic trash bag. Tie the bag tightly. Place the bag on the ground in the testing area. Weigh down the bag with a rock.
3. Have your teacher use an electric drill to create holes in the sides and bottom of the clear, plastic container. Place one of each type of garbage in the container. Place the container on the ground in the testing area. Secure any objects that could be blown away by the wind with rocks.
4. Place a third sample of each type of garbage in an empty shoe box. Keep this box in a dark, dry, and cool indoor location. You may wish to wrap a garbage bag around this box to contain odors.
5. Create an observational scale from 1–10 to determine the percentage of decomposition. For example, 1 is 0% decomposed, 5 is 50% decomposed, and 10 is 100% decomposed.
6. Record observations of each piece of garbage on the data table.
7. Record weekly observations of all three samples of garbage. Describe the size, shape, and color of the garbage in each sample. Use the observational scale to determine the percentage of decomposition for each individual piece of garbage.
8. Repeat step 7 on the same day each week for 10–12 weeks.

NAME_______________________________________DATE_______________

TALKING TRASH

EXPERIMENTAL DESIGN

A large majority of the trash we produce is deposited into landfills and buried. It may take hundreds of years for some types of garbage, like soft drink bottles and plastic bags, to decompose. Many of these items can be recycled for other uses and save space in landfills.

TASK: Design an experiment to determine how the long it takes for garbage not exposed to natural elements to decompose compared to garbage exposed to natural elements, such as wind, rain, and heat from the sun. Complete the worksheets (pages 10–14) as you design and perform your Talking Trash experiment.

HINTS

HYPOTHESIS:

- Think about what you already know about the trash items you chose and how well they might decompose. You may want to conduct further research on landfills and the materials that you chose.

VARIABLES, CONTROL, AND CONSTANTS:

- What will you test?
- What will change as a result of the independent variable?
- To which trial will you compare all of the results?
- Which parts of the experiment must stay the same?

GRAPH:

- Create a graph that shows a picture of the data you collected in this experiment. Remember to label both axes and give the graph an appropriate title.

MEET BRIAN FISHER

SPOTLIGHT ON SCIENTISTS

When rain falls to the ground, the water does not stop moving. Some water flows into streams or lakes, some is used by plants, some returns to the atmosphere through evaporation, and some sinks into the ground.

Groundwater is water that is found underground in the cracks and spaces in soil, sand, and rock. Groundwater is stored in—and moves slowly through—layers of soil, sand, and rocks called **aquifers**. Aquifers typically consist of gravel, sand, sandstone, or fractured rock, like limestone. These materials have large connected spaces that allow water to flow through them. The speed that groundwater flows depends on the size of the spaces in the soil or rock and how well the spaces are connected.

Brian Fisher is a **groundwater and environmental geologist** for the city of Wichita, Kansas. His job is to monitor the local groundwater and soil for signs of contamination that could affect human health and the environment. Recently, the city of Wichita found an area of contamination that was $2\frac{1}{2}$ miles long and $1\frac{1}{2}$ miles wide! Mr. Fisher helped set up a computerized groundwater contamination water treatment plant that will clean the groundwater and soil in this area. The plant has 12 pumping wells that will clean 920 gallons of water per minute. But, because groundwater moves so slowly and it is difficult to clean soil beneath the water table, it will take almost 60 years to clean up this site!

Mr. Fisher also helps home owners solve water problems. Shallow groundwater may release vapors that may effect the quality of the air and cause health problems. Other people call him to find the depth of groundwater so that private wells can be dug for lawn and garden watering. He once received a phone call from a woman who said that her hair had turned orange! After testing her water, he discovered that a type of bacteria in her well was causing the trouble.

In this activity, you will simulate how chemicals can enter and contaminate groundwater and soil.

MATERIALS:

- glass baking dish
- cherry- or grape-flavored powdered drink mix
- large book
- sand
- spray bottle filled with water
- spoon

PROCEDURE

1. Fill the glass dish with sand about 1" (2.54 cm) deep.
2. Scoop out a small hole in the sand at one end of the dish.
3. Fill the hole with the powdered drink mix and cover the powder with more sand.
4. With the book, prop up the end of the glass dish that contains the powdered drink mix about 2" (5.08 cm).
5. Use the spray bottle to thoroughly wet the sand. You will need to continuously mist the sand for several minutes.
6. Carefully raise the glass dish. Look carefully at the bottom of the dish. Draw your observation of the soil contamination in the box on page 64.

EARTH SCIENCE

NAME____DATE____________________

Draw your observations of the soil contamination in the box below.

Answer the following questions in complete sentences.

1. What happened to the colorful powder and surrounding sand after they were thoroughly misted with water?

____

____

____

2. What might have caused this to happen?

____

____

____

3. What can you infer about groundwater contamination from your observation?

____

____

____

TRY THIS! Write a letter to the editor of your local newspaper about your position on groundwater contamination. Do you think this is something that people in your community should be concerned about? Why or why not? Share your letter with your classmates.

DIGGING FOR THE PAST

SCIENCE IN SOCIETY

Scientists who learn about Earth's people and past by studying **artifacts** and **fossils** are called **archaeologists** and **paleontologists**. Archaeologists look for clues to learn how past cultures lived so that we can understand more about how present people live and adapt to the environment. Using a process called **carbon dating**, paleontologists can estimate the age of fossils. They can determine the age of the rock layer where the fossil was found, which helps scientists date the other material that is found at that level. Without fossils, we would have a much more incomplete picture of Earth's early history.

Removing artifacts and fossils from the ground can be a long and tedious process, so when archaeologists find one, they must be patient. In this activity, you will use a model to see how difficult and time-consuming it is to remove artifacts and fossils from the surrounding rock.

MATERIALS:

- plastic bones
- shells
- bottle caps
- paper clips
- shoe box
- plaster of paris
- petroleum jelly
- cotton swabs
- plastic spoons
- paintbrush
- metal spoon
- toothbrush

PROCEDURE

1. Choose a variety of items from the materials your teacher has provided. These will be the "artifacts" and "fossils." Using a cotton swab, completely cover each object with a thin layer of petroleum jelly.
2. Prepare the plaster of paris according to the package directions.
3. Fill the shoe box halfway with plaster of paris. Place the artifacts and fossils in different locations and depths in the plaster of paris.
4. Allow the plaster of paris in the shoe box to dry overnight.
5. Trade shoe boxes with another group. Use the metal spoon, paintbrush, and toothbrush to carefully excavate the artifacts and fossils from the shoe box. These objects are often delicate and can be easily damaged, so work slowly!

On another piece of paper, answer the following questions in complete sentences.

1. What was the most difficult part of excavating the artifacts and fossils?
2. What was the easiest part of excavating the artifacts and fossils?
3. How is this activity similar to what a paleontologist experiences? How is it different?

TRY THIS! Choose one of the artifacts or fossils that you discovered in your shoe box. Write a story about the object. What was it used for? How old is it? How did it become buried in the ground? Share your story with the class.

NAME ______________________ DATE __________

PROBLEM SOLVING

SCIENCE SKILLS

A **paleontologist** is a scientist who studies **fossils** to learn about the history of Earth. Sometimes, when paleontologists find a fossil, they only have a few bones to help them determine the type of animal they have found. From these bones, they also try to learn what the animal ate, where it lived, and how it died. This requires them to use their **problem-solving** skills.

MATERIALS:

- envelope of "fossilized remains" puzzle pieces

PROCEDURE

1. Remove one "fossilized remains" puzzle piece from the envelope and study it carefully. Try to determine what type of animal is in the picture.
2. On the data table below, write the name of the animal you think is pictured on the whole puzzle.
3. Continue to draw puzzle pieces, one at a time, from your envelope. After examining each piece, record your guess of the animal's name on the data table. When you are sure of the animal's identity, write your final guess and circle it. Then, remove the rest of the pieces and put together the puzzle.

DATA TABLE:

Guess	Animal Name	Guess	Animal Name
1		8	
2		9	
3		10	
4		11	
5		12	
6		13	
7		14	

On another piece of paper, answer the following questions in complete sentences.

1. How is this activity similar to the work of a paleontologist?
2. Do you think it would be more difficult to identify more than one animal from the same envelope? Why or why not?
3. How do you think a paleontologist can determine so many things about an animal, such as where it lived, what it ate, or how it died, from only one or two bones?

EARTH SCIENCE

IF FOSSILS COULD TALK!

THE "WRITE" STUFF

When paleontologists find a fossil, they may only have a few bones or footprints from which to draw conclusions about how an animal lived and died. They must also rely on a strong background knowledge of other organisms and environments.

In this activity, you will make predictions about several types of fossils that might actually be found by a paleontologist. Think about the following questions as you look at each picture.

1. Was the animal a mammal, reptile, bird, or fish?
2. Did the animal live in water or on land? Did the animal fly?
3. Did the animal eat plants or other animals? Was it an herbivore, omnivore, or carnivore?
4. Did the animal live in a warm climate or cool climate?
5. Can you tell if the animal was eaten by a predator? Did it die in a fight with another animal or of natural causes?

Choose two of the fossils pictures below. On another piece of paper, write your answers to the questions above in complete sentences. Remember, scientists are not always sure whether their answers are right or wrong. They can only use their background knowledge and problem-solving skills to make their best predictions!

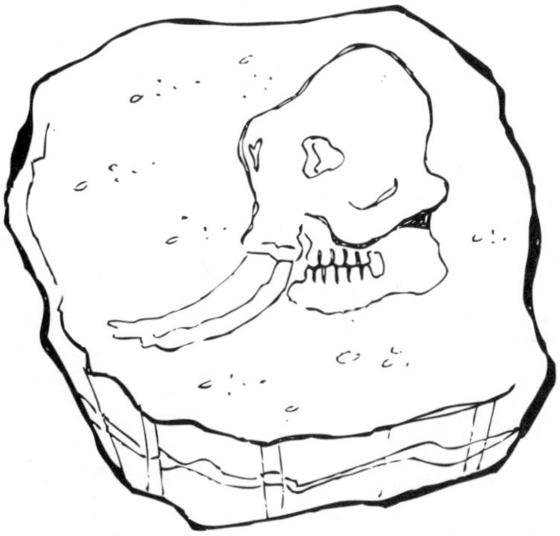

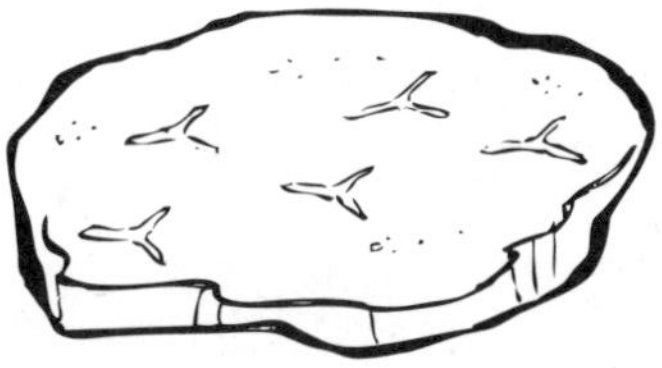

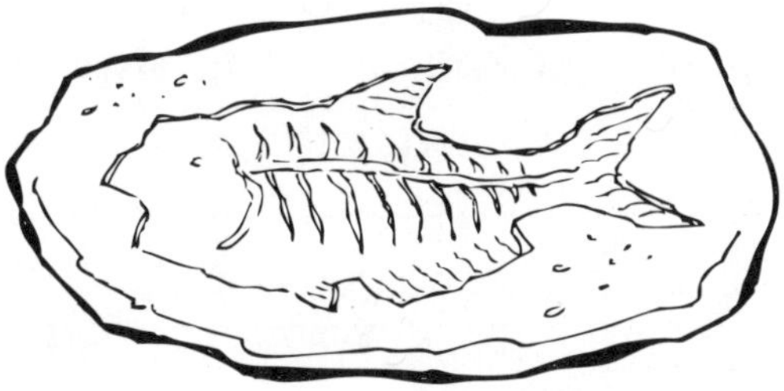

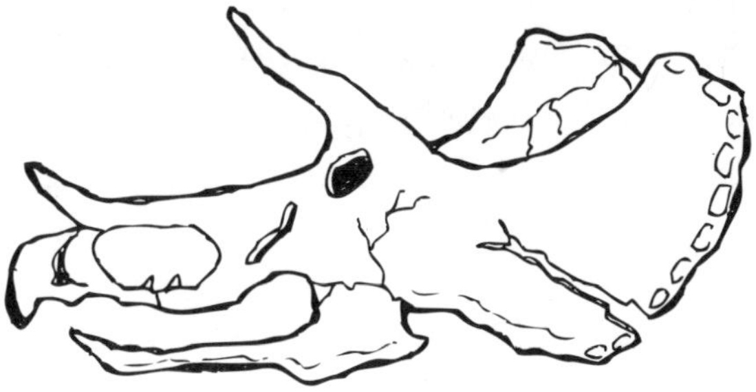

EARTH SCIENCE

HURRICANE HOUSE

ENGINEERING CHALLENGE

The earth processes we see today, including erosion, movement of plates, and changes in the atmosphere, are similar to those that have occurred in the past. Earth history is influenced by occasional catastrophes, such as the destructive forces of hurricanes. Some scientists believe that the actions of humans have caused a rise in temperature on Earth, which may increase the number and severity of these storms.

Engineers have attempted to design structures that withstand the forces of these types of storms, such as homes in Pensacola Beach, Florida, that are built in the shape of large concrete domes. Many homes are designed to structurally withstand hurricane-force winds and storm surges.

CHALLENGE: Construct a miniature house on a "beach" that can withstand the destructive winds and water surge of a model hurricane.

MATERIALS:

- craft sticks
- aluminum foil
- plastic wrap
- small rocks
- small sticks and twigs
- balsa wood
- plastic interlocking blocks
- wooden interlocking logs
- any additional teacher-approved materials
- paper clips
- string
- duct tape
- glue
- large plastic tub
- sand
- pie tin
- electric fan
- water

EARTH SCIENCE

GUIDELINES

1. Use science books, encyclopedias, or the Internet to research buildings that are designed to withstand the forces of hurricanes.
2. Use the sand to construct the "ocean floor" and "beach" inside the plastic tub. Choose from the materials to construct your group's miniature house on the beach.
3. Once you have finished house construction, fill the plastic tub with 5" (12.7 cm) of water. Simulate crashing waves by pushing and pulling the water back and forth using the pie tin. Larger waves can be created by placing the pie tin deeper in the water and increasing the stroke length. Simulate strong winds by placing the electric fan at the end of the tub, opposite the model house.

Answer the following questions on another piece of paper.

1. Draw a diagram and write a paragraph that describes your group's miniature house. Explain the features that will help it withstand the forces of the simulated hurricane. List the materials you used and why you chose those materials.
2. Describe what happened to your group's model house during the hurricane simulation.

PANGAEA PUZZLE

JUST THE FACTS

Millions of years ago, Earth was a very different place. Since that time, climates changed, and different species have emerged, evolved, and become extinct. Landforms also changed dramatically. In 1912, a scientist named Alfred Wegener introduced his theory of continental drift when he noticed the continents could be pieced together like a rough puzzle. The continents fit together to form one large continent that Wegener called **Pangaea**.

Earth's crust is broken into many pieces. These pieces are called **plates**. There are 12 main plates on Earth's surface that slide very slowly on the mantle's upper layer. Over time, the plates have slowly changed positions and have moved the continents into their present-day locations. The plates are still moving very slowly, at a rate of $^1/_2$" (1.27 cm) per year.

Cut out the seven present-day continents below. Then, try to piece them together to form the continent of Pangaea. Be aware that the continents will not fit together exactly. Over millions of years, as the level of the ocean has varied, it has also eroded and changed the coastlines of the continents.

CREATING CRATERS SAMPLE EXPERIMENT

QUESTION: How does the height from which an object is dropped affect the width and depth of the impact crater it creates?

HYPOTHESIS: If the height from which an object is dropped affects the width and depth of the impact crater it creates, then an object dropped from a greater height will create a wider and deeper impact crater.

VARIABLES, CONTROL, AND CONSTANTS:

Independent variable: Height from which the object is dropped

Dependent variable: Width and depth of the impact crater created

Control: Dropping an object from a low height (50 cm)

Constants: Variables that must remain the same

- size, mass, and shape of object
- angle at which the object is dropped
- type and shape of substance in which the object lands
- measurement tools
- method of measurement

MATERIALS:

- 5 cups of moist sandbox sand
- spherical object (golf ball or marble)
- permanent marker
- baking sheet
- meterstick
- masking tape
- chair

PROCEDURE

1. Place 5 cups of moist sandbox sand on the baking sheet. Shape the sand into a small mound. Flatten the top of the mound.
2. Place the baking sheet and sand mound on the floor, next to a wall.
3. Use the meterstick to measure a height of 50 cm from the floor. Place a small piece of masking tape at this height on the wall. Label it 50 cm.
4. Repeat step 3 for the heights of 100 cm, 150 cm, 200 cm, and 250 cm.
5. Hold the ball at the 50 cm mark, directly above the center of the mound. Drop the ball into the sand mound. Remove the ball and carefully measure the width and depth of the impact crater created by the ball. Record this data on the data table.
6. Fill in the crater made by the ball and repeat step 5 two additional times. Find the average width and depth of the impact crater made by a ball dropped from 50 cm.
7. Repeat steps 5 and 6 for each of the other heights (100 cm, 150 cm, 200 cm, and 250 cm). You may need to stand on the chair to hold the ball for the greater heights.

NAME________________________________ DATE____________

CREATING CRATERS

EXPERIMENTAL DESIGN

A **meteoroid** is a rock or mineral, that comes from an asteroid or comet that is orbiting the sun. As it enters Earth's atmosphere, it creates a streak of light, called a **meteor**, or shooting star. **Meteorites** are pieces of the meteoroid that have survived their passage through Earth's atmosphere and fall onto Earth's surface.

When a meteoroid impacts with Earth, it forms a crater. Fifty thousand years ago, a small iron meteoroid fell to Earth near Winslow, Arizona, and created what is now called Barringer Crater. The meteorite that survived its passage through the atmosphere was about 40' (39.6 m) in diameter, but it produced a crater that is 4,000' (1,219 m) in diameter and 660' (220 m) deep! About 120 impact craters have been identified on Earth so far.

TASK: Design an experiment about how the height from which a meteor falls affects the width and depth of the crater it forms. Complete the worksheets (pages 10–14) as you design and perform your Creating Craters experiment.

HINTS

HYPOTHESIS:

- Think about what you already know about meteoroids, meteors, meteorites, craters, motion, and forces. You may want to research meteorites that have landed on Earth and created craters.

VARIABLES, CONTROL, AND CONSTANTS:

- What will you test?
- What will change as a result of the independent variable?
- To which trial will you compare all of the results?
- Which parts of the experiment must stay the same?

GRAPH:

- Create a graph that shows a picture of the data you collected in this experiment. Remember to label both axes and give the graph an appropriate title.

NAME____DATE______________

MEET DR. GRETCHEN JONES

SPOTLIGHT ON SCIENTISTS

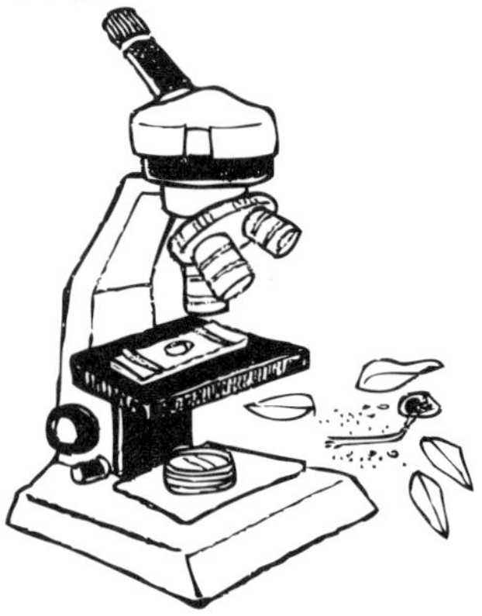

Dr. Gretchen Jones is a **palynologist** for the Areawide Pest Management Research Unit at the United States Department of Agriculture. A palynologist is an expert on pollen and spores. **Pollen** is a powder-like substance used by plants to reproduce. In one way, pollen grains are like snowflakes because each species of plant has a unique type of pollen grain. Dr. Jones keeps this in mind when she is studying insect pests. When an insect lands on a flower, pollen will often stick to the insect's legs and body. By observing an insect very closely, Dr. Jones can tell where it has been!

Palynologists can also help other scientists learn about plants and animals that lived at different times throughout Earth's history. They can examine pollen grains preserved in lake mud and determine the climate and types of plants that grew in that area. Dr. Jones has helped paleontologists examine the soil around prehistoric Native American burial sites to find which plants were used in the burials. She has also used her problem-solving skills to help the police prove that some honey in New Zealand was illegally imported from China!

In this activity, you will model how pollen can be easily spread from place to place.

MATERIALS:

- paper dots (from a hole punch)
- blank piece of paper

PROCEDURE

1. Pour the paper dots on the floor near the entrance door of your classroom. These paper dots will represent pollen.
2. Do not intentionally move any of the dots. Throughout the day, take note of where the "pollen" goes and how it gets there.
3. At the end of the school day, draw a map of your classroom. Label the locations where pollen can be found. If pollen is found in the hallway or other locations around your school, extend your map to show the location of these pollen grains.

1. The dots represent pollen. What represents insects or animals? How can you tell if your pollen was carried to a different "country"?

____

____

2. Why would it be helpful for a palynologist to be familiar with the pollen of plants from all over the world?

____

____

NAME ______________________ DATE __________

MISSION MEASUREMENT

SCIENCE SKILLS

In 1999, engineers at NASA made what might seem to be a small mistake when they sent a spacecraft to study Mars. The engineers on Earth that operated the rockets propelling the spacecraft used customary units of measurement (feet, pounds, gallons). But, the engineers who programmed the spacecraft before it launched used metric units (meters, grams, liters). This may not seem like a big deal until you look at the consequences of their actions. The difference in the units of measurement caused the spacecraft to travel too quickly, and it crashed into the surface of Mars! In order to prevent something like this from happening again, engineers are now very careful to use the same units of measurement.

In this activity, you will practice the skill of **converting metric measurements**. Your task is to work as an engineer in a group to build a structure. Each student will be given a card with a set of partial directions. The teacher will assign groups based on these directions. All directions are necessary to build the structure successfully. You may only use the ruler provided on the side of this page to measure the lengths of objects.

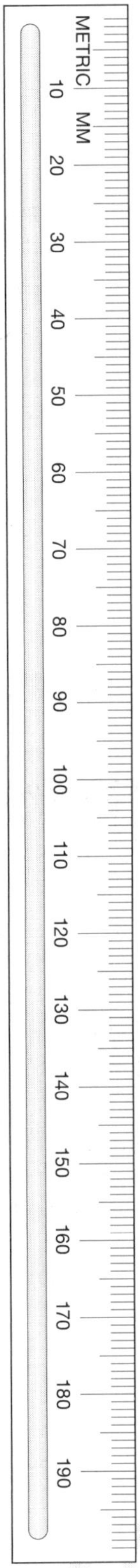

EARTH SCIENCE

MATERIALS:

- plastic foam cup
- tissue paper
- hole punch
- instruction cards provided by teacher
- metric ruler on the side of this page
- scissors
- tape
- paper clips
- string
- metric balance

1. What was the most difficult part of creating the structure?

____

____

2. What was the easiest part of creating the structure?

____

____

3. How is this activity similar to what an engineer at NASA experiences? How is it different?

____

____

____

ENGINEER 1:

1. Cut off the top part of the plastic foam cup so that it is 3.5 cm high.
2. Draw four dots that are equal in distance from each other on the outside rim of the cup.
3. Measure 3 grams of paper clips and place them in the cup.

10 mm	= 1 cm
1,000 mm	= 1 m
100 cm	= 1 m
1,000 m	= 1 km

ENGINEER 2:

1. On the tissue paper, draw a rectangle that measures 312 mm on two sides and 0.228 m on the other two sides.
2. Use the hole punch to punch a hole in each corner of the tissue paper. The holes should measure exactly 2.1 cm from each corner to the center of each hole.

10 mm	= 1 cm
1,000 mm	= 1 m
100 cm	= 1 m
1,000 m	= 1 km

ENGINEER 3:

1. Cut four pieces of string that measure 0.000293 km each.
2. Attach each string to the tissue paper by tying one end of each string through each hole.
3. Tape the other end of each string to a dot on the cup rim. Make sure that the strings do not cross when you attach them to the cup.

10 mm	= 1 cm
1,000 mm	= 1 m
100 cm	= 1 m
1,000 m	= 1 km

TEAM INSTRUCTIONS:

1. Use the ruler to measure a height of 2 meters on a wall. Mark this height with a piece of masking tape. Drop the structure from this height.
2. Brainstorm ways to improve the design. How would you change the structure so that it would fall slower or faster or be able to change directions? How could you improve the design so that it could hold more paper clips and still fall at the same speed?

NAME____DATE______________________

OUT OF THIS WORLD VOCABULARY

JUST THE FACTS

Write each letter in the correct blank to match each word with its definition. Use a dictionary, a science book, or the Internet to complete this activity.

1. ________ asteroid
2. ________ comet
3. ________ star
4. ________ satellite
5. ________ planet
6. ________ great red spot
7. ________ orbit
8. ________ rotation
9. ________ axis
10. ________ constellation

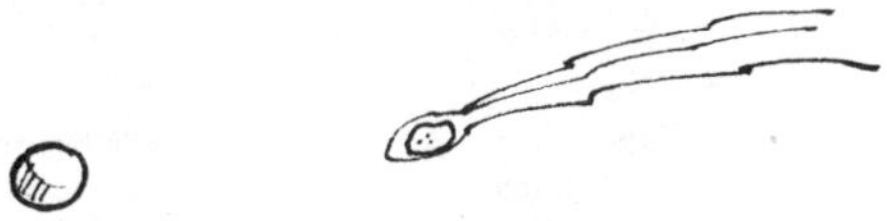

a. an object that orbits a planet or a moon

b. a closed circle path that an object takes as it revolves around another object

c. an imaginary straight line around which a planet turns; this line through Earth goes through the north and south poles

d. when an object turns around a central point or on its axis

e. rocky or metal objects that orbit the sun in a belt between Mars and Jupiter; also called planetoids or minor planets

f. a huge ball of glowing gas that can exist for billions of years; our sun is the closest one

g. a group of stars that form a pattern; there are 88 that can be seen from Earth

h. a small object orbiting the sun that is made of frozen ice, gas, and dust; it has a tail that always points away from the sun

i. a large body that orbits a star and does not produce its own light; there are nine in our solar system

j. a huge, long-lasting storm in the atmosphere of Jupiter near its equator; it is the biggest storm in this solar system

EARTH SCIENCE

NAME________________________DATE____________

PLANETARY EXPLORATION

THE "WRITE" STUFF

NASA has sent robotic orbiters and rovers to explore eight of the nine planets in our solar system, but there is still much we do not know about our neighbors in space!

Use science books, encyclopedias, or the Internet to research the nine planets. On another piece of paper, list at least three interesting facts about each planet. Then, write a persuasive letter to NASA that describes which planet you think should be explored in the next robotic mission. Include several reasons for choosing this planet and describe what you hope to learn from the mission.

NAME____DATE___________________

MARTIAN LANDING GEAR

ENGINEERING CHALLENGE

In 2004, NASA sent two rovers to Mars to explore the planet's surface and search for evidence of water. Designing the landing gear for these rovers was a difficult challenge because the rovers needed to be protected as they dropped slowly onto the planet's surface.

CHALLENGE: Design a landing device that can keep a rover, represented by a raw egg, from breaking when dropped from a height of at least 10' (3.05 m).

MATERIALS:

- raw egg
- trash bag
- tape
- paper clips
- chenille craft sticks
- straws
- plastic foam cups
- craft sticks
- string
- sheets of newspaper
- paper towels
- balloons
- meterstick
- any additional teacher-approved materials

GUIDELINES

1. Brainstorm with your group several designs for the egg landing device you will build using the materials listed above. Remember to design the device so that the egg can be easily removed—you do not want to break the egg while removing it from heavy packaging!
2. Decide on one design and draw and label a picture on another piece of paper.
3. Gather your materials and construct your device.
4. Drop your device from a height of at least 10' (3.05 m). If the egg does not break, repeat the experiment but increase the height of the drop. If the egg breaks, redesign the egg landing device and try again.

1. Describe how the landing device your group created protected the raw egg from breaking.

____

____

____

2. How could the design of your group's device be improved? What additional materials would you use?

____

____

____

EARTH SCIENCE

MOON PHASES SAMPLE EXPERIMENT

QUESTION: From the perspective of an observer, how does the amount of visibly illuminated surface of an object (illuminated from a light source), change as the object revolves around a second object?

HYPOTHESIS: If, from the perspective of an observer, the amount of visibly illuminated surface of an object changes as it revolves around a second object, then when the object is between the observer and the light source, the visible surface of the object will be completely dark.

VARIABLES, CONTROL, AND CONSTANT:

Independent variable: The day that the moon is observed

Dependent variable: As seen from Earth, the amount of the moon's surface seen from Earth that is illuminated by light from the sun

Control: The day when none of the moon's lit surface can be seen from Earth (new moon)

Constant: Variable that must remain the same

- location of the observer

MATERIALS:

- binoculars or telescope (optional)

PROCEDURE

1. Create a three column data table to record your moon observations. In the first column, you will record the date. In the second column, you will write a description of your observations. In the third column, you will draw the moon's appearance.
2. Each day or night, locate the moon in the sky. The time of day the moon appears in the sky will change over the course of the month. On the data table, describe whether the moon's face appears to have grown larger or smaller since the previous day's observation. Draw a picture of the moon's appearance. If it is too cloudy to observe the moon, record that information on the data table, as well.
3. When the moon appears to return to the same appearance as when you began the observations, count the number of days it took to complete the lunar cycle.
4. Repeat steps 1–3 two additional times.

NAME______________________________ DATE______________

MOON PHASES

EXPERIMENTAL DESIGN

Have you ever noticed that each night the moon's shape appears to change? Throughout history, various cultures have used these changes, called **moon phases**, to mark the passing of time. Most people assume that the moon goes through a complete cycle of phases once per month. However, all of the months do not contain the same number of days.

Exactly how many days does it take for the moon to complete one cycle of its phases? While today it may be easy to look up the answer to this question in a book or on the Internet, ancient astronomers found the answer by making observations.

TASK: Design an experiment to determine the number of days it takes for the moon to complete one cycle of its phases. Complete the worksheets (pages 10–14) as you design and perform your Moon Phases experiment.

HINTS

HYPOTHESIS:

- Think about what you already know about how the moon's appearance changes and how long it takes for the moon to complete a full lunar cycle.

VARIABLES, CONTROL, AND CONSTANTS:

- What will you test?
- What will change as a result of the independent variable?
- To which trial will you compare all of the results?
- Which parts of the experiment must stay the same?

DATA TABLE:

- Create a data table that describes the data you collected in this experiment. You may want to draw pictures of the moon as it changes its phases.

EARTH SCIENCE

NAME________________________________DATE____________

EARTH AND MOON CROSSWORD

JUST THE FACTS

Use the vocabulary terms from the word bank below to complete the crossword puzzle.

WORD BANK

lunar eclipse	day	revolution	elliptical	waning
equinox	solar eclipse	year	new moon	tilt
rotation	full moon	waxing	maria	sphere

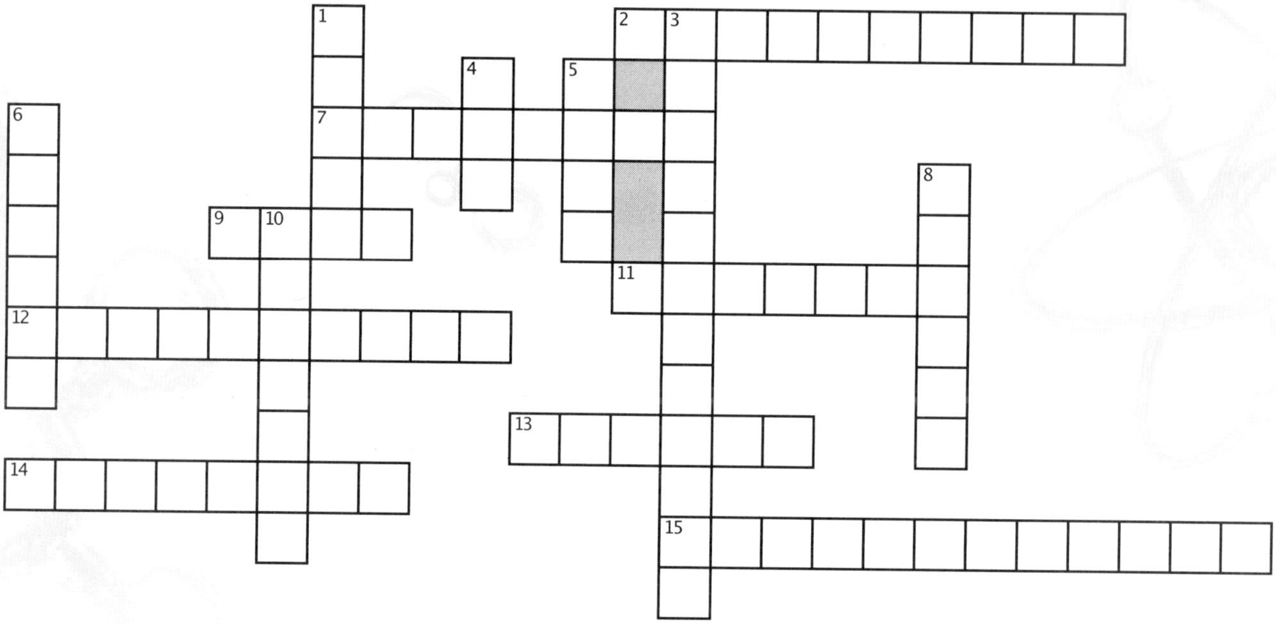

ACROSS

2. shape of Earth's orbit around the sun
7. spinning of Earth on its axis
9. time it takes for Earth to move around the sun one time
11. moon phase in which none of the moon's lighted surface can be seen
12. Earth's yearly orbit around the sun
13. phase of the moon's cycle when the amount of the lit face is increasing
14. moon phase in which all of the moon's lighted surface can be seen
15. occurs when the moon moves directly between Earth and the sun; blocks part of the sun's light from reaching Earth

DOWN

1. dark-colored regions of lava on the surface of the moon
3. occurs when Earth's shadow falls directly on the moon
4. time it takes for Earth to spin once on its axis
5. cause of the seasons
6. The shape of Earth is a ____________.
8. phase of the moon's cycle when the amount of the lit face is decreasing
10. hours of daylight and darkness are equal on this day

NAME________________________DATE____________

FUTURE SPACE MISSIONS?

SCIENCE IN SOCIETY

Funding a space program is expensive, and many astronauts have risked their lives traveling into space to increase scientific knowledge. On January 28, 1986, seven astronauts lost their lives when the space shuttle *Challenger* was destroyed in a tragic accident. In February 2003, another seven astronauts did not return when the space shuttle *Columbia* broke apart 16 minutes before landing.

However, there are also numerous benefits to a space program. Technology created for space exploration has helped make advances in communication with cellular phones and satellites, traveling by airplanes at high speeds, weather warning systems, and artificial heart technology. The Hubble telescope allows scientists to view previously unknown distant galaxies. Other people simply believe the spirit of exploration is a reason to continue the space program.

Use science books, encyclopedias, or the Internet to research spaceflight and exploration. Complete the T-chart below with pros and cons for continuing the space program. Then, on another piece of paper, organize your information into a report describing these different points of view. You may also include your own ideas about whether to continue the spaceflight and exploration program.

PROS	CONS

MEET DR. ROSALY LOPES

SPOTLIGHT ON SCIENTISTS

Ever since she was a young girl, Rosaly Lopes knew she wanted to study the solar system. At the time, her home country of Brazil did not have a space program, so she knew she would eventually have to leave. Her parents were very supportive of her decision to study in a foreign country. At the age of 18, she moved to England to study planetary sciences and later accepted a job at NASA's Jet Propulsion Laboratory in Pasadena, California.

Not only has Dr. Lopes traveled all over Earth studying active volcanoes, she has also specialized in volcanoes on other planets and moons in our solar system. During the *Galileo* mission, she discovered 71 new volcanoes on Jupiter's volcanically active moon, Io. She has also studied the similarities and differences between volcanoes on Mars and Earth.

In this activity, you will become a volcanologist and create a model of a volcano. Then, you will take core samples of the areas of the volcano's eruptions.

MATERIALS:

- 4 different colors of play dough
- baking soda
- vinegar
- large piece of corrugated cardboard
- graduated cylinder
- measuring spoon
- paper cup
- clear drinking straws
- permanent marker
- ruler
- paper towels

EARTH SCIENCE

PROCEDURE

1. Cut the top off of the paper cup so that it is 1¼" (3.175 cm) high. Place it in the middle of the cardboard.
2. Place one level tablespoon of baking soda into the cup and add 4 tsp (20 mL) of vinegar. You have just created a model volcanic eruption!
3. Watch as the "lava" spills over the edges of the cup. When the eruption is over, use the permanent marker to draw a line around perimeter of the lava flow. Clean off the lava flow from the cardboard with a paper towel.
4. Spread a layer of one color of the play dough over the cardboard inside the perimeter of the line drawn for the lava flow.
5. Empty the paper cup and repeat steps 2–4 three additional times. Each time, mark the perimeter of the lava flow and cover the area with play dough. The play dough should form several layers over previous eruptions.
6. To understand when and how different eruptions have occurred, geologists often take core samples of the surrounding area. Take core samples of the eruptions by sticking clear drinking straws into four different locations around the cardboard. Pull out the straws and study the colorful layers. Can you tell in which order the eruptions occurred?

NAME____DATE______________________

DATA TABLE: Draw the core samples taken from the four different locations in the area surrounding your volcano.

Location 1	Location 2	Location 3	Location 4

Answer the following questions in complete sentences.

1. How can you determine the order in which each eruption occurred by looking at core samples?

____

____

2. Why did some of the core samples contain all four colors, while others may have only contained two or three?

____

____

3. Why was it important to take core samples in several locations, rather than from only one location?

____

____

4. How were the model eruptions you created similar to real volcanic eruptions? How were they different?

____

____

TRY THIS! Research volcanoes that are found on other planets, such as Mars, and moons, such as one of Jupiter's moons, Io.

LIFE SCIENCE TEACHER TIPS

Spread of Disease (page 88)

You will need one disposable cup per student. Before class begins, mark the bottom of one cup with a small X. Fill each cup about half full of water. In the cup marked with the X, secretly dissolve 2 teaspoons of baking soda. The baking soda and water mixture represents the bacteria or virus that will "infect" the rest of the students.

Place all of the cups on a tray and hand one cup to each student in the class. Then, follow the procedure on page 88.

After students have "shaken hands" with their classmates and tested their cups of water, have them carefully look at the bottoms of their cups for the small X. The X indicated the person who was "sick" first. Do not reveal this until the end of the activity!

Have students answer the questions. Then, lead a discussion about the transfer of illness. Try to trace the path of the bacteria/virus transmission through the class.

Growing Bacteria (page 89)

Petri dishes and nutrient agar may be purchased from a scientific supply company. Petri dishes with agar should be prepared several days before this activity.

Most bacteria collected in the environment will not be harmful. However, once the bacteria multiply into millions of colonies in a petri dish, they become more of a hazard. Be sure to protect open cuts with rubber gloves and never ingest or breathe in growing bacteria. Keep growing petri dishes taped closed until your experiment is complete.

Before disposing of dishes in the trash, the bacteria should be destroyed. Pour a small amount of household bleach over the colonies while holding each petri dish over the sink.

Create a Cell Model (page 93)

Caution: Before completing any food activity, ask families' permission and inquire about students' food allergies and religious or other food preferences.

Encourage students to use a variety of materials to create their cell models. Students may also create edible cell models that can then be shared with their classmates.

Create a Mechanical Arm (page 95)

A mechanical arm can be made to resemble a large pair of practice chopsticks or tweezers. Create a fulcrum by folding a piece of paper several times. Place the fulcrum between two dowels, one-third of the distance from the ends. Secure it in place with a rubber band or tape. Use the long ends of the dowels to pick up objects by pulling the short ends of the dowels away from each other.

Observing Animal Behavior (page 97)

Caution: Before completing any nature activity, ask families' permission and inquire about students' plant and animal allergies. Remind students not to touch plants or animals during the activity.

You can easily provide animals for student observations by purchasing crickets or worms from a pet supply store. These are a good choice for observation since they can be released outside when students have finished the activity. Ask to borrow other teachers' classroom pets, such as guinea pigs, fish, or mice.

Discuss observations and assumptions as a class. Everyone should agree with observations, but not everyone will agree with others' assumptions. Explain that this is okay. Scientists regularly debate the meanings of their observations, and they often conduct experiments to find additional information about the topic in question.

Worm Preferences (page 100)

Earthworms may be purchased at bait shops, sporting goods stores, or pet stores. If you plan to keep the earthworms over a longer period of time, they should be fed weekly. To feed the worms and not alter a second variable in the ongoing experiment, equal masses of used coffee grounds and chopped vegetables can be spread over each type of soil in the baking dish.

Animal Intelligence (page 101)

An animal intelligence testing device can be created using a cereal box, string, scissors, and an analog clock. This device could be used to test whether an animal can tell time or if it relies on instinct to know it is time to be fed.

1. Lay a cereal box on its back. Place an analog clock beside the long edge of the box.
2. Cut a small "door" in the box by cutting three sides of a rectangle into the top of the box, leaving the fourth side as the hinge for the box.
3. Poke a small hole near the edge of the door opposite the hinge. Thread a piece of string through the hole and tie a knot large enough for the string to stay in place.
4. Position the analog clock so that the minute hand is pointing away from the cardboard box, perpendicular to the box.
5. With the door open, tie the other end of the string to the end of the clock's minute hand. The string should be pulled taught, and the excess string should be removed.
6. As the minute hand moves around the clock, the tension on the string will allow the door to open and close.

Design a Closed Ecosystem (page 109)

For this investigation, each group of students will need a large bottle that can be stoppered or sealed airtight. Aquatic plants, such as elodea and zostera, may be purchased at a pet or aquarium supply store.

1. Place 2" (5 cm) of soil in the bottom of the container and cover it completely with 1/4" (0.6 cm) of sand.
2. Slowly and carefully pour water into the container. The water should not disturb the sand and expose the soil underneath. Fill the container to 1/4" from the top. Allow the water to dechlorinate for 48 hours before adding plants to the ecosystem.
3. Plant a few pieces of aquatic plant by pushing them below the sand into the soil with a piece of wire or long fork.
4. Seal the container with the lid or stopper. Apply a bead of silicone caulk or duct tape around the lid to create a seal.
5. Position the ecosystem on a windowsill or under the 100-watt lightbulb.
6. Observe the closed ecosystem over a few weeks and change the position of the lighting until the system is balanced.

Follow the Trail (page 113)

Ant food gathering provides an opportunity for students to observe a form of animal communication. Ants use pheromone trails to lead colony members to food sources. Be sure to encourage students to simply observe the ants and not harm them in any way.

Animal Activity Levels (page 119–120)

Caution: Before completing any nature activity, ask families' permission and inquire about students' plant and animal allergies. Remind students not to touch plants or animals during the activity.

Meet Vaughn Weaver (page 123)

A water filter can be created by using plastic cups, cheesecloth, coffee filters, and rubber bands.

1. Poke several small holes into the bottom of a plastic cup. While holding the cup over a larger plastic container, pour a small amount of sludge water into the cup. Larger particles (gravel, small sticks) will remain in the cup. Pour the resulting filtered water into a plastic cup.
2. Secure a piece of cheesecloth onto the open end of a plastic cup with a rubber band. Hold the cup over a larger plastic container and pour the filtered water from step 1 through the cheesecloth. Smaller particles (sand, coffee grounds) from the sludge water will remain on top of the cheesecloth, while water passes into the plastic cup.
3. Remove the cheesecloth. Pour the filtered water into another cup.
4. Secure a coffee filter to the open end of another plastic cup with a rubber band.
5. Pour the filtered water through the coffee filter. Additional small particles from the filtered water will remain on top of the coffee filter. The filtered water will pass through the filter into the cup.

NAME________________________________DATE______________

CONTROLS AND VARIABLES

JUST THE FACTS

Experiments usually begin with questions such as, "Will a mouse run faster through a maze if music is playing?" or "Does fertilizing a plant affect the size of its leaves?"

Let's use the second question as an example. If you wanted to find out whether fertilizing a plant affects the size of its leaves, you could set up an experiment to find out. You would begin with two identical plants. Then, you would water the first plant with plain water only. This is called a **control**. By watering the first plant without fertilizer, you will have something with which to compare the second plant that will be fertilized.

Before you water the second plant, add fertilizer to the water. Water the second plant with the water and fertilizer mixture. The fertilizer is called a **variable**. The variable is what you are changing in your experiment. There are also other possible variables, but those variables must remain **constant**. For example, both plants should receive the same amount of water and soil, be planted in the same type of pot, and be placed in the same sunny location. If you do not keep the other variables constant, they could affect the outcome of your experiment. You would not really know which variable was actually causing the change in the size of the plant's leaves.

Of course, no experiment is perfect. Since mistakes can be made, it is always best to conduct an experiment several times. This is known as doing more **trials**. If you get the same results with each trial, you can be more confident that your findings are correct.

Design an experiment based on each of the following questions.

EXPERIMENT 1: Will talking to a plant increase its height?

To conduct this experiment, I would: ____

____

____

____

____

The **control** in this experiment is: ________________________________

The **variable** in this experiment is: ________________________________

The variables that I must keep **constant** for this experiment are: ______________

____

____

LIFE SCIENCE

NAME_______________________________________ DATE_______________

EXPERIMENT 2: How does heat affect the distance a rubber band can be stretched?

To conduct this experiment, I would: ____

____

____

____

____

The **control** in this experiment is: ____

The **variable** in this experiment is: ____

The variables that I must keep **constant** for this experiment are: ____________________

____

____

____

EXPERIMENT 3: Do crickets chirp more often when they are near other crickets?

To conduct this experiment, I would: ____

____

____

____

____

The **control** in this experiment is: ____

The **variable** in this experiment is: ____

The variables that I must keep **constant** for this experiment are: ____________________

____

____

____

LIFE SCIENCE

NAME________________________________DATE______________

SPREAD OF DISEASE

SCIENCE IN SOCIETY

Have you ever had the chicken pox or a sinus infection? Behind these illnesses are microorganisms called **bacteria** and **viruses**. Bacteria and viruses invade your body through your nose, eyes, mouth, or cuts in your skin. Some are easily spread from one person to another. In order to see how easily bacteria and viruses can be spread from person to person, try the following activity.

MATERIALS:

- red litmus paper
- water in disposable cups (provided by the teacher)

PROCEDURE

1. Pretend you are at a party where you do not know very many people. To "shake hands" with someone, empty your cup into his cup. Then, have him pour the entire contents of his cup back into your cup. Finally, split the water between the two cups so that you each have a cup that is half full.
2. Move on to "shake hands" with someone else at the party. After five minutes, you should have had contact with at least four other students.
3. Test your water with the red litmus paper. If the paper remains red, you are free from "illness." If it turns blue, you have come in contact with someone who is "ill," and you are likely to "get sick."

1. How many people started out with the illness? ______________________________

2. How many people "caught" the illness? ______________________________

3. Not everyone who contracted the illness exchanged water with the original person who had the illness-causing bacteria or virus. How do you think he managed to catch it?

____

____

4. What have you learned about the spread of illness from this activity?

____

____

____

THINK ABOUT THIS: How can you prevent yourself from getting sick, even if you have come into contact with someone or something carrying a bacteria or virus?

LIFE SCIENCE

NAME________________________ DATE____________

GROWING BACTERIA

SCIENCE SKILLS

Even though you cannot see them, bacteria are everywhere! They are commonly found on objects many people come into contact with as well as in places that are not cleaned often. In this activity, you will practice your **scientific observation** skill as you grow a bacteria sample. On another piece of paper, make a list of areas around your school you think might contain a large population of bacteria.

MATERIALS:

- 2 petri dishes with nutrient agar
- cotton swabs
- wax pencil

PROCEDURE

1. Choose two of the areas you listed to test for bacteria.
2. You will receive two petri dishes. The first will remain closed as your **control**. Do not remove the cover of this petri dish.
3. The second petri dish is your **variable**. Turn it upside down on a table. Draw a line on the bottom of the dish with a wax pencil, dividing it into two halves. Label one side with the name of one area you plan to test and label the other side with the name of the second area. Write the names of the sample areas below.
4. Rub a cotton swab over a surface in the first testing area. Remove the cover from the second petri dish and lightly rub the cotton swab on the half of the dish labeled with that area.
5. Repeat step 4 with a clean cotton swab for the second testing area.
6. Close the dish and place it in a warm, dry area. Check for bacteria every day for three days. Bacteria will look like discolored spots in the dish. If you have a fuzzy substance, it is probably mold.

Draw your petri dish each day in the spaces below.

DAY 1 DAY 2 DAY 3

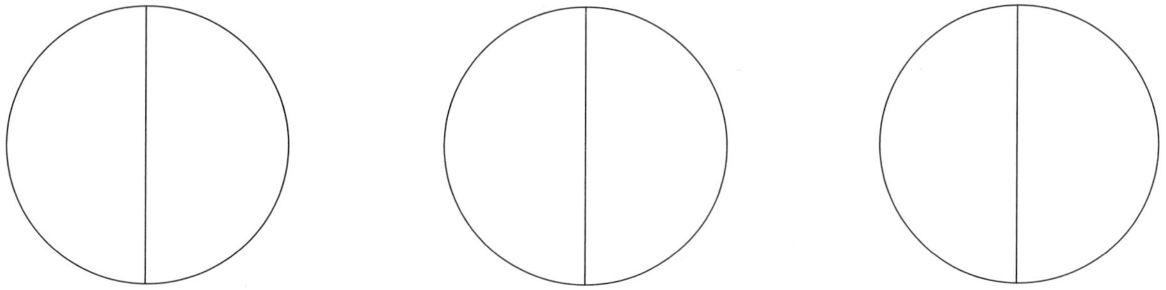

Sample Area 1: ____________________ Sample Area 2: ____________________

On another piece of paper, answer the following questions in complete sentences.

1. Which areas of your school have the most bacteria? How do you know?
2. Why did you use a clean cotton swab to take each sample?

ANTIBACTERIAL SOAP SAMPLE EXPERIMENT

QUESTION: How effective are antibacterial soaps in controlling the growth of bacteria colonies?

HYPOTHESIS: If introducing soap to a bacteria colony grown in a petri dish affects its growth, then applying antibacterial soap to a bacteria colony will destroy the greatest amount of bacteria.

VARIABLES, CONTROL, AND CONSTANTS:

Independent variable: Type of soap applied to bacteria colonies

Dependent variable: The amount of bacteria colony growth after applying soap

Control: A bacteria colony not exposed to any soap

Constants: Variables that must remain the same

- location of bacteria sample
- size/type of petri dish
- volume of nutrient agar in petri dish
- measurement tools
- method of measurement

MATERIALS:

- 3 disposable petri dishes with nutrient agar
- antibacterial liquid soap
- regular liquid soap
- distilled water
- 3 cotton swabs
- wax pencil
- 2 plastic cups
- magnifying glass
- measuring cups
- measuring spoons
- 2 eyedroppers
- transparent tape

PROCEDURE

1. Use the wax pencil to label the bottom of the first petri dish *C* for control. Label the second petri dish *R* for regular soap. Label the third petri dish *A* for antibacterial soap.
2. Choose an area in the school from the Growing Bacteria activity (page 89) that was a successful surface from which to obtain a bacteria sample. Rub a cotton swab over this surface. Remove the cover from the first petri dish and lightly rub the cotton swab in the agar. Close the dish.
3. Repeat step 2 two additional times for the second and third petri dishes. Use a clean cotton swab for each sample. Tape the *C* petri dish closed.
4. In a plastic cup, dilute one teaspoon of regular soap in one cup of distilled water.
5. Open the lid of the *R* petri dish. Use an eyedropper to add one drop of the regular soap solution to the bacteria sample. Tape the *R* petri dish closed.
6. Repeat step 4 with the antibacterial soap. Open the lid of the *A* petri dish. Use the second eyedropper to add one drop of the antibacterial solution to the bacteria sample. Tape the *A* petri dish closed.
7. Each day for five days, use the magnifying glass to examine the petri dishes without opening them. Record daily observations on the data table. Describe the size, shape, and color of the bacteria in each colony.

NAME____DATE____________________

ANTIBACTERIAL SOAP

EXPERIMENTAL DESIGN

Have you ever gotten a cut and been told to wash it with antibacterial soap? This type of soap is designed to stop the growth of any bacteria that might have been on your skin or on the object that cut you before it can get inside your wound. People often depend on these soaps to prevent infection, but do they really work?

TASK: Design an experiment to determine whether antibacterial soaps can stop the growth of bacteria. Complete the worksheets (pages 10–14) as you design and perform your Antibacterial Soap experiment.

HINTS

HYPOTHESIS:

- Think about what you already know about bacteria and antibacterial soaps. You may want to research several different types of bacteria and how antibacterial soaps prevent bacteria from growing.

VARIABLES, CONTROL, AND CONSTANTS:

- What will you test?
- What will change as a result of the independent variable?
- To which trial will you compare all of the results?
- Which parts of the experiment must stay the same?

DATA TABLE:

- Record daily observations on the data table. Develop a scale for the amount of living bacteria in the sample throughout the experiment.

LIFE SCIENCE

NAME________________________________DATE______________

CELLULAR CROSSWORD

JUST THE FACTS

Use the vocabulary terms from the word bank below to complete the crossword puzzle. Use science books, encyclopedias, or the Internet to complete this activity.

WORD BANK:

cell wall	cell membrane	cytoplasm	nucleus
lysosome	mitochondria	DNA	chloroplast
vacuole	Golgi bodies		

ACROSS

2. responsible for packaging molecules and transporting them to other parts of the cell
4. contains chlorophyll in a plant cell
5. the code of our genetic material
9. double layer that surrounds a cell, allows materials in and out of a cell
10. destroys worn-out cell parts and bacteria that get inside of a cell

DOWN

1. provides the energy for a cell, often called the cell's "powerhouse"
3. All parts of the cell are located within this liquid, which is mostly water.
6. control center of the cell, contains DNA
7. maintains the shape of a plant cell
8. In plant cells, these large organelles hold water and wastes. They are much smaller in animal cells.

CREATE A CELL MODEL

SCIENCE SKILLS

In this activity, you will **create a model** of a plant or animal cell. Label the parts of your model using pins and small strips of paper. On another piece of paper, create a data table to record the required information for your cell model.

MATERIALS:

- buttons
- different shapes, sizes, and colors of pasta
- small plastic bags
- vegetable oil
- bottle caps
- beads
- chenille craft sticks
- plastic cups and bowls
- small strips of paper for labels
- pins for labels
- any additional teacher-approved materials

DATA TABLE INFORMATION

- Type of cell (plant or animal)
- Names of cell's structures
- Functions of cell's structures
- Type of material used to create each cell structure
- Reasons that you chose to use these materials to create the cell's structures

LIFE SCIENCE

NAME________________________________DATE______________

COMPARING CELLS

THE "WRITE" STUFF

Use science books, encyclopedias, or the Internet to complete this graphic organizer about the similarities and differences between plant and animal cells. Then, on another piece of paper, organize the facts into a paragraph that compares and contrasts plant and animal cells.

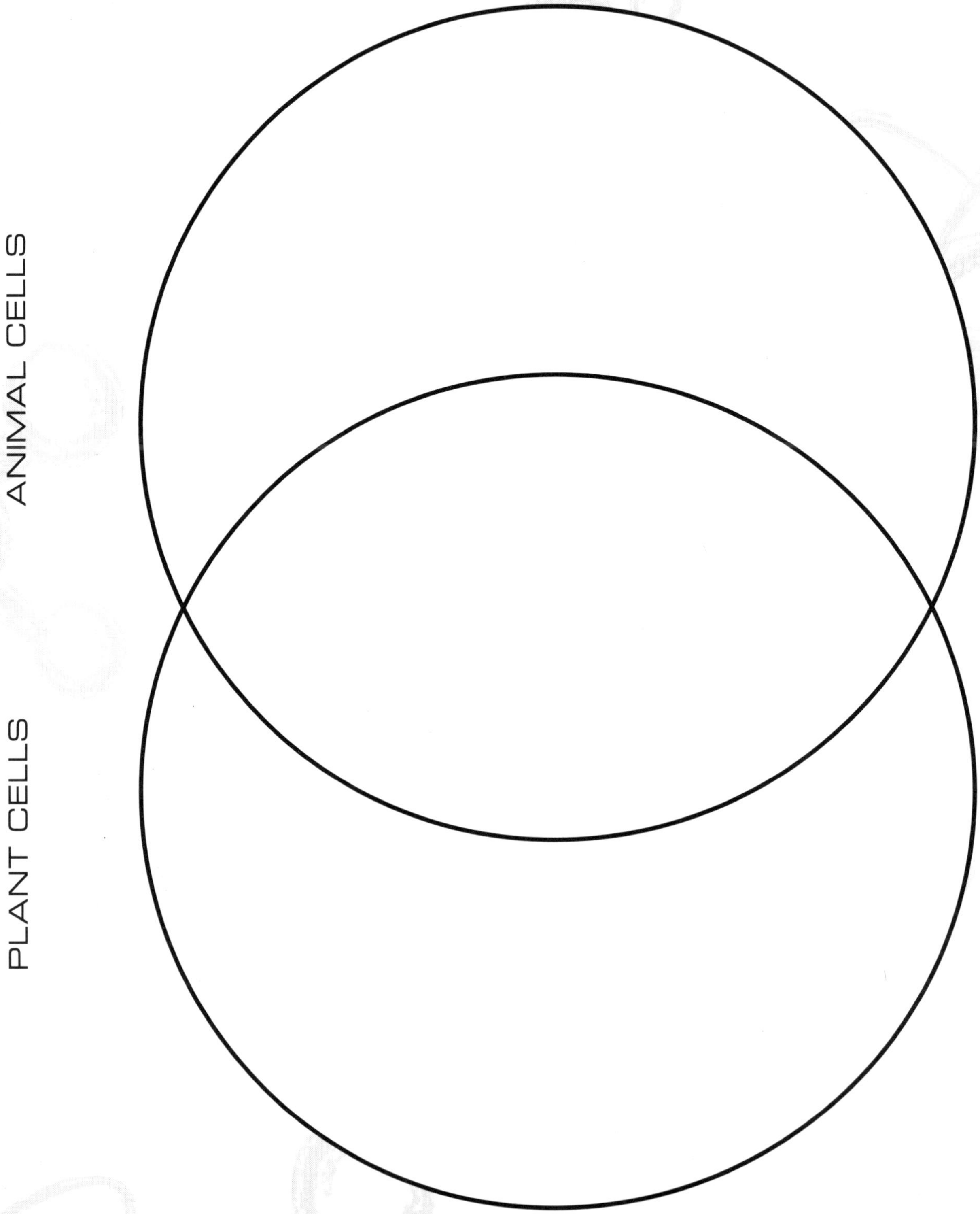

NAME_______________________________ DATE______________

CREATE A MECHANICAL ARM

ENGINEERING CHALLENGE

The human body is an amazing machine! It is made of millions of cells that all work together to perform the functions that allow us to walk, run, breathe, and eat. The human body is also fragile and can be injured. Sometimes, after a bad accident, a person may have to have an arm or leg **amputated**, or removed from the body, because it is injured too badly to heal. Other times, a person may be born missing a limb due to a birth defect. Engineers have invented mechanical arms and legs to help these people perform normal daily activities, such as brushing their teeth or walking up stairs.

CHALLENGE: Work in a group to design a mechanical arm that can pick up a bottle of glue.

MATERIALS:

- craft sticks
- string
- masking tape
- paper towel tubes
- wooden dowels
- poster board
- straws
- any additional teacher-approved materials
- plastic cups
- rubber bands
- paper clips
- wrapping paper tubes
- plastic bottles
- chenille craft sticks
- thumbtacks
- glue

GUIDELINES

- The operator of the mechanical arm must remain at a distance of at least 3' (91 cm) from the bottle of glue.
- The mechanical arm must be at least 2' (61 cm) in length.
- The mechanical arm must be able to pick up the bottle and move it a distance of at least 12" (30.48 cm).
- On another piece of paper, draw and label a picture of the mechanical arm your group designed.

Write a paragraph that describes how your group's mechanical arm works.

____

____

____

____

____

____

MEET DR. CHERYL NICKERSON

SPOTLIGHT ON SCIENTISTS

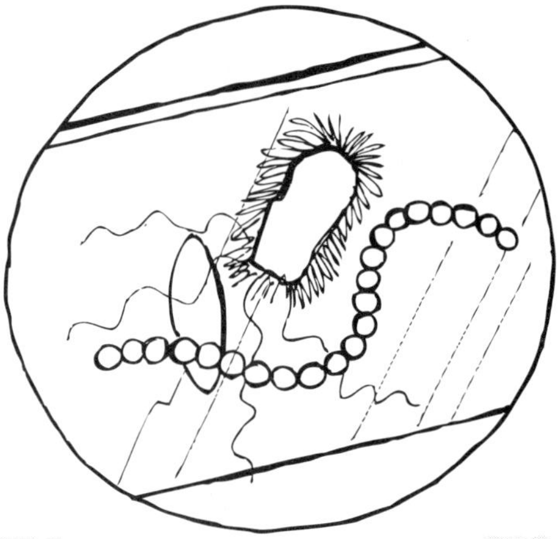

A **microbiologist** looks at organisms too small to be seen with the naked eye. Microbiologists usually study these organisms through a microscope, and it is their job to explore the ways in which these tiny creatures affect the lives of humans.

Dr. Cheryl Nickerson is a member of the microbiology and immunology faculty at Tulane University in New Orleans, Louisiana. She chose to study microorganisms because she wanted to understand how such tiny creatures could cause such terrible diseases in humans. Through her research, she hopes to enhance the quality of human life.

One of her current projects is the study of how **microgravity** affects the growth of bacteria. Microgravity is an environment with very little gravity, such as space or the moon. Dr. Nickerson's research has shown that salmonella bacteria, which can make people very ill on Earth, attack the body in greater numbers when grown in simulated microgravity. Her research is important to the health of astronauts, especially those living onboard the space station for long periods of time.

Someday, scientists hope to send human beings to Mars. Since this trip could take as long as two years, scientists need to be concerned about the astronauts becoming ill during their travels. The more information doctors have about how bacteria grow in space, the better prepared they will be to treat sick astronauts.

If you are interested in microorganisms, you may want a career in microbiology. There are many different types of microbiologists.

- bacteriologist
- biotechnologist
- cell biologist
- immunologist
- parasitologist
- virologist
- epidemiologist
- mycologist

Choose one of the microbiology careers from the list above and use science books, encyclopedias, or the Internet to research this type of microbiologist. Create a poster to present to the class that includes a written description and drawings or pictures of the kind of work this type of scientist does.

NAME________________________DATE______________

OBSERVING ANIMAL BEHAVIOR

SCIENCE SKILLS

One of the best ways to learn about an animal is to observe it in action! Scientists observe an animal by watching it closely and taking notes on its behavior, or what the animal is doing. An **observation** is a fact that other scientists would agree upon if they witnessed the same behavior. Observations can be detailed descriptions of the animal's physical characteristics, where it is sitting or sleeping, or the way it moves.

Making an observation is not always as easy as it sounds. Sometimes people can be biased about the behavior of an animal based on their own feelings and experiences. For example, when you hear a bird singing, you might believe the bird is happy. Even though happiness is a human emotion, many people assign emotions to animals. In fact, scientists who study bird behaviors have determined that a bird will sing for a variety of reasons, including designating its territory or announcing its presence to a mate. By believing the bird is happy, you have made an **assumption**. This means you have taken an observed fact (the bird is singing) and formed an opinion about why it is behaving a certain way. While it is not always wrong to make assumptions, it is important to realize that animals are not necessarily ruled by the same emotions that motivate people.

To learn the difference between an observation and assumption, you will observe a live animal. Write detailed observations of the animal's behavior in the data table below. If you are watching more than one animal, notice how the animals interact with each other.

Then, try to determine why the animal displayed each behavior you observed. Write your assumption for each observation in the data table below.

Observations	Assumptions
1.	
2.	
3.	
4.	
5.	
6.	
7.	
8.	

LIFE SCIENCE

NAME______________________________DATE__________

OBSERVATION vs. ASSUMPTION

JUST THE FACTS

Decide whether each statement is an observation or an assumption. Write *O* for observation or *A* for assumption on each blank below.

Example: O—The dog wagged its tail. A—The dog was glad to see me.

1. ________ The rabbit moved toward the apple slice.
2. ________ The rabbit is curious about the apple slice.
3. ________ The rabbit is hungry.
4. ________ The crickets are in the corner of the cage.
5. ________ The crickets are afraid.
6. ________ The crickets are chirping.
7. ________ The mice touched noses when first placed in a cage together.
8. ________ The mice were saying hello to each other.
9. ________ The snake flicked its tongue in and out when food was placed in its cage.
10. ________ The snake was happy to see the food.
11. ________ There is a snakeskin in the corner of the cage.
12. ________ The skin came from the snake in the cage.
13. ________ The chameleon changed from brown to green when placed on the grass.
14. ________ The mealworm is not moving.
15. ________ The mealworm is tired.
16. ________ The mealworm is napping.
17. ________ The mealworm spent most of its time on the green construction paper.
18. ________ Mealworms like the color green more than any other color.
19. ________ The fish are lonely.
20. ________ The fish stayed in the left side of the aquarium for a total of five minutes.

WORM PREFERENCES SAMPLE EXPERIMENT

QUESTION: How does an organism's preference for the conditions of its natural environment affect its choice for the conditions of an artificial environment?

HYPOTHESIS: If the conditions in a location affect an organism's preference of location, then an organism will prefer to stay in a location that most resembles its natural environment.

VARIABLES, CONTROL, AND CONSTANTS:

Independent variable: Amount of moisture in each type of soil

Dependent variable: Number of worms found daily in each type of soil

Control: Dry soil

Constants: Variables that must remain the same

- type/amount of potting soil in each side
- number of sprays of water to moisten the soil
- temperature of soil
- amount of time between locating worms

MATERIALS:

- 4 earthworms
- large, deep, rectangular baking dish
- potting soil
- spray bottle with water
- hand shovel
- 2 white index cards
- large piece of cardboard to cover the baking dish
- metric ruler
- pencil

PROCEDURE

1. Use the hand shovel to fill the baking dish with potting soil 1" (2.54 cm) from the top.
2. Label the first index card *moist soil*. Place this index card in front of the left half of the baking dish.
3. Label the second index card *dry soil*. Place this index card in front of the right half of the baking dish.
4. Place the pencil on top of the soil to separate the two types of soil.
5. Spray the soil on the left side of the baking dish 50 times with the spray bottle. Make sure the soil on this side of the baking dish is thoroughly wet.
6. Place four worms on the pencil in the center of the baking dish.
7. Cover the baking dish completely with the piece of corrugated cardboard. This will block any light from entering the dish.
8. Each day, uncover the dish. Carefully, use your fingers to dig through the soil in each side of the dish. Count the number of worms found in each type of soil. Record the results on the data table. Then, place the four worms back in the center of the dish.
9. Replace the cardboard cover to block light from entering the baking dish. Once a week, repeat step 5 to maintain the moisture level of the moist soil.
10. After one week, find the average number of worms found in each type of soil.

NAME____DATE______________

WORM PREFERENCES

EXPERIMENTAL DESIGN

Have you ever noticed that you have certain **preferences** about your environment? You might have a preference for complete silence rather than background noise while you study. You might have a preference for bright colors rather than plain white walls in your bedroom.

Animals also have preferences. Your dog might prefer one certain sleeping spot over another. A fish might prefer to hide in weeds rather than to swim in open water. Even smaller animals, like mice and insects, have preferences when it comes to choosing their environments.

TASK: Design an experiment to determine whether earthworms have a preference for moist soil or dry soil. Complete the worksheets (pages 10–14) as you design and perform your Worm Preferences experiment.

HINTS

HYPOTHESIS:

- Think about what you already know about earthworms and where they live. You may want to research earthworms and their environments.

VARIABLES, CONTROL, AND CONSTANTS:

- What will you test?
- What will change as a result of the independent variable?
- To which trial will you compare all of the results?
- Which parts of the experiment must stay the same?

GRAPH:

- Create a graph that shows a picture of the data you collected in this experiment. Remember to label both axes and give the graph an appropriate title.

LIFE SCIENCE

NAME______________________________DATE______________

ANIMAL INTELLIGENCE

ENGINEERING CHALLENGE

Scientists have often debated whether certain animals are intelligent. One of the criteria used to determine if an organism is intelligent is its ability to solve problems. For example, some seeing-eye dogs know when it is safe to lead blind people across busy streets. A meerkat, a small African mammal, has a special "language" for alerting others about predators, such as snakes and jackals.

Some scientists have created devices for testing animal intelligence. For example, when scientists want to know if mice could solve problems, they created a large maze. The scientists put a mouse in the maze to see if it could find food at the end.

CHALLENGE: Use the materials listed below to construct a model of a device that will test the level of an animal's intelligence.

MATERIALS:

- craft sticks
- cereal boxes
- paper clips
- string
- duct tape
- glue
- plastic interlocking blocks
- wooden interlocking logs
- paper clips
- aluminum foil
- plastic wrap
- small rocks
- small sticks and twigs
- analog clock or timer
- any additional teacher-approved materials

GUIDELINES

- Some animals to consider testing for intelligence include mice, hamsters, gerbils, lizards, dogs, cats, or snakes.
- The animal intelligence device does not need to be a working model, but you should be able to explain how it works to the class.
- On another piece of paper, draw and label a diagram of the device your group designed.

Write a paragraph that describes how your group's animal intelligence device works.

____

____

____

____

____

____

NAME____ DATE____________________

ANIMAL DEFENSES

JUST THE FACTS

Animals and plants respond to danger in many different ways. Some plants are poisonous. Many animals use bites or stings to protect themselves. Others have evolved shells or hard outer skeletons to defend against predators. Some animals use camouflage to hide from danger.

Choose three of the animals or plants below. Use science books, encyclopedias, or the Internet to research the behaviors and defenses evolved by these animals and plants to respond to danger or predators. Record your research below.

Turtle

Rabbit

Chameleon

Poison Ivy

Walking Stick

Scorpion

King Cobra

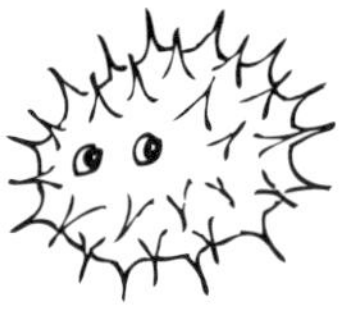
Puffer Fish

Killdeer

Jellyfish

1. Name of organism: ____

   Defense: ____

2. Name of organism: ____

   Defense: ____

3. Name of organism: ____

   Defense: ____

ENDANGERED SPECIES INTERVIEW

SCIENCE IN SOCIETY

In order to survive in a changing environment, an organism needs to find resources, such as food and water; be able to grow and reproduce; and avoid being eaten by predators. Many plant and animal species have survived in their habitats for millions of years, while others are not able to adapt to the rapid changes brought on by humans. These changes include habitat destruction, the introduction of new species, poaching, and pollution.

Pretend you are a reporter and conduct an interview with an endangered species. You may choose a species from the list below or choose your own. Use science books, encyclopedias, or the Internet to research the species. Then, write an interview with your endangered species that answers the questions below.

Have a partner help you present your interview to the class as a skit. You may also want to dress as the endangered species you researched.

ENDANGERED SPECIES:

- African elephant
- blue whale
- Florida panther
- giant panda
- American alligator
- gopher tortoise
- giant armadillo
- Red Hills salamander
- whooping crane
- Alabama sturgeon
- black rhino
- California condor

INTERVIEW QUESTIONS

1. What is the name of the endangered species?
2. Is the animal a mammal, reptile, amphibian, bird, fish, or insect?
3. Is the animal a carnivore, herbivore, or omnivore?
4. What does the animal eat? Does it need a specific type of food?
5. Is the animal a predator, prey, or both?
6. Where does the animal live? What does it use for shelter?
7. Why is the species endangered? Why is it having difficulty surviving in its environment?
8. What can humans do to help protect the species?
9. Why is it important to protect the species?
10. Write three additional questions for the endangered species to answer.

NAME________________________________DATE____________

YOU BE THE ZOOLOGIST

JUST THE FACTS

A **zoologist** is a scientist that studies animals. Many zoologists work for zoos and help determine what kinds of habitats are needed by the animals that live there.

Contact a zoologist or use science books, encyclopedias, or the Internet to research how the behavior of an animal in captivity is different from the behavior of that animal in the wild. Find out how zoologists use animal behavior to design a habitat. How have zoos tried to make the habitat similar to the natural habitat of each animal?

In this activity, you will design an animal habitat for a zoo. Choose an animal that is commonly found in a zoo and research its natural habitat. Then, in the space below, design an artificial habitat for that animal. Keep in mind how important it is to provide an environment as close as possible to what that animal experiences in the wild.

On another piece of paper, write a paragraph describing how you have tried to make this zoo habitat similar to the animal's natural habitat.

LIFE SCIENCE

NAME______________________________DATE______________

ZOO PROS AND CONS

THE "WRITE" STUFF

Millions of people visit zoos each year to view animals they would not ordinarily be able to see. However, there is controversy over whether zoos are good places for animals to live. While zoos often protect endangered species, they also restrict the space in which animals roam and do not provide a natural environment for each animal.

Use science books, encyclopedias, or the Internet to research zoos. Complete the T-chart below with pros and cons for keeping animals in artificial habitats in zoos. Then, on another piece of paper, organize the information into a report describing these different points of view. You may also include your own ideas for improving the lives of animals living in zoos around the world.

PROS	CONS

NAME________________________________ DATE____________

MEET DR. PATRICK GANNON

SPOTLIGHT ON SCIENTISTS

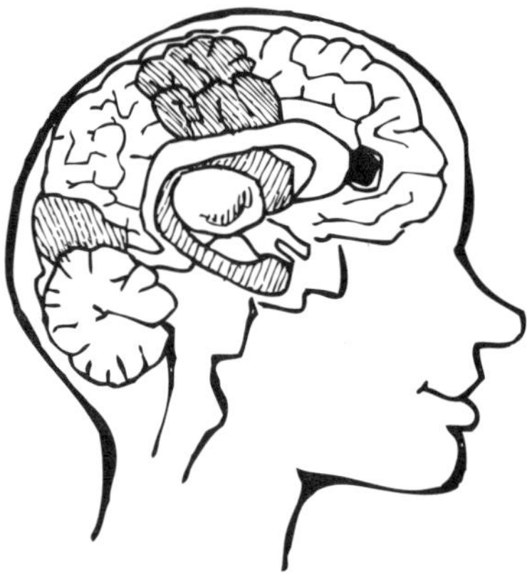

Dr. Patrick Gannon is an **otolaryngologist** at the Mount Sinai School of Medicine in New York, New York. An otolaryngologist is a person who studies the ear, nose, throat, and neck areas. Dr. Gannon's research involves the study of language differences between chimpanzees and humans, and he is part of a groundbreaking investigation into the physiological reasons for those differences.

The ability of human beings to communicate through complex spoken language is an important feature that separates us from other animals. Scientists currently understand that language is controlled by a special area in the brain. This area, called the **planum temporale,** is larger in the left hemisphere than it is in the right hemisphere. However, Dr. Gannon has discovered that this same trend occurs in the brains of chimpanzees. This discovery has changed the way we think about the areas that control language in the brain.

Since humans and chimpanzees have almost 99% of their DNA in common, scientists wonder why chimps do not have a spoken language similar to ours. Chimps use facial, hand, and body movements to communicate with each other, instead of the complex voice inflections and words used by humans. This could mean that the planum temporale is related to the use of gestures and visual communication as a type of modern day "chimpanzee language." A larger left planum temporale in the common ancestor of humans and chimpanzees, some six million years ago, may have allowed humans to evolve a spoken language. Dr. Gannon and his team will continue to study chimpanzee brains in order to find an answer.

Scientists have tried communicating with chimpanzees and apes using sign language. Some scientists have had success with a very famous gorilla named Koko. This gorilla seems to have learned to use American Sign Language to communicate with humans.

Use science books, magazines, or the Internet to research Koko's sign language communication. Then, write three questions that scientists could ask Koko to decide whether she can understand sign language. Share your questions with the class.

1. ____

____

2. ____

____

3. ____

____

LIFE SCIENCE

NAME ______________________ DATE ____________

CLASSIFICATION

SCIENCE SKILLS

When scientists place organisms into groups according to the organisms' similarities or differences, it is called **classification**. Classification enables scientists to organize information, identify types of organisms with ease, or study the way groups of organisms interact. In this activity, you will practice your classification skills with a collection of buttons.

MATERIALS:

- container of 20 buttons of different sizes, shapes, and colors
- ruler
- metric balance

PROCEDURE

1. Closely examine each button in the container. On another piece of paper, create a data table to record each button's size, shape, and color. Also, measure and record the length, width, and mass of each button.
2. Create three groups of buttons based on a particular similarity you notice. Name each group based on this common characteristic (for example, round, square, and oval). Write the name of each group in Column 1 of the chart below.
3. Divide each of the first three groups into two smaller groups based on another similarity. Name each of these groups based on this common characteristic. Write the names of these groups in Column 2 below.
4. Share the reasons for the classifications you created with the class.

Column 1 **Column 2**

TRY THIS! It is not uncommon for scientists to have difficulties classifying organisms. On another piece of paper, write a paragraph describing some of the difficulties you had while classifying the buttons in this activity.

NAME _______________________ DATE ____________

CLASSIFYING ANIMALS

JUST THE FACTS

All organisms on Earth are grouped into one of six **kingdoms**: Animals, Plants, Protists, Fungi, Eubacteria, and Archaebacteria. Each of these kingdoms is further classified into smaller groups based on their similarities and differences.

Animals can be classified as **vertebrates** or **invertebrates**. Animals with backbones are vertebrates, and animals without backbones are invertebrates.

Animals may also be classified as **herbivores**, **omnivores**, or **carnivores**, depending on what they eat. Herbivores eat only plants. Carnivores eat only other animals. Omnivores eat both plants and animals.

Animals can be further classified as **warm-blooded** or **cold-blooded**, depending on how their body temperatures are controlled. A warm-blooded animal's body temperature usually does not change. A cold-blooded animal's body temperature changes with its surroundings.

Use science books, encyclopedias, or the Internet to research the animals pictured below. First, label each animal as either a *vertebrate* or *invertebrate*. Then, write if the animal is a *carnivore*, *herbivore*, or *omnivore*. Finally, label each animal as either *warm-* or *cold-blooded*.

African Lion

Praying Mantis

Human

Striped Bass

Bald Eagle

Cobra

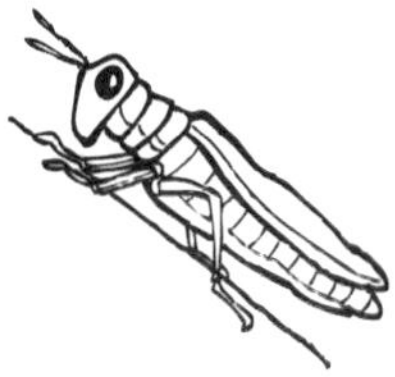

Grasshopper

Grizzly Bear

NAME______________________________________ DATE________________

DESIGN A CLOSED ECOSYSTEM

ENGINEERING CHALLENGE

Many scientists have compared Earth to a spaceship traveling around the sun. Everything needed to survive is on this planet, including food, water, air, and shelter. Our planet recycles the air we breathe, the water we drink, and the ground on which we walk. When you look at the way our planet works, it is truly amazing that this all happens naturally.

In this activity, you will design a system that provides the same sustainable environment as the planet Earth. This system is called a **closed ecosystem**. An ecosystem consists of living organisms (plants, animals, and microorganisms) that interact with each other and with the environment in which they live (soil, climate, water, and light).

CHALLENGE: Work in a group to design an aquatic ecosystem that can support plant life. Use the materials listed below to build the ecosystem.

MATERIALS:

- large, clean, glass jar with lid
- potting soil
- all-purpose sand
- aquatic plants (elodea or zostera)
- stiff wire or long fork
- light source (sunlight or 100-watt lightbulb)
- duct tape or silicone caulk
- ruler

GUIDELINES

1. Your teacher will provide aquatic plants to use in your ecosystem.
2. The ecosystem cannot receive food, water, or air from an outside source. (It can receive sunlight or light from a lightbulb.)
3. Use science books, encyclopedias, or the Internet to research closed ecosystems.
   - Decide how your group will construct the ecosystem.
   - How many plants will you include?
   - How much soil, sand, and water you will use?
   - Brainstorm other things you will need to know in order to support the plants that will live in the closed ecosystem.

Write a paragraph describing how you designed the closed ecosystem. Describe how it will support living organisms. If needed, continue your answer on another piece of paper.

____

____

____

____

____

____

NAME____DATE______________

RAIN FOREST PRODUCTS

SCIENCE IN SOCIETY

Earth's rain forests, often called the "lungs of our planet," play a very important role in the health of our planet. They once covered 14% of Earth's land surface, but now they only cover 6%. Some scientists believe that the last remaining rain forests could be destroyed in less than 40 years.

Animals and plants of the rain forest provide the basis for many products we use every day. New animals and plants are being discovered, but some important animals and plants are lost forever by the destruction of the rain forests. The loss of the undiscovered plants and animals means the loss of many useful products.

All of the products listed below originally came from areas in or near a rain forest. Look at the list below. Place a check mark next to each product you or your family uses.

1. ________ bamboo
2. ________ balsa wood
3. ________ teak furniture
4. ________ sandalwood
5. ________ rosewood
6. ________ mahogany
7. ________ jute twine
8. ________ burlap
9. ________ rubber tires
10. ________ chicle (chewing gum base)
11. ________ rice
12. ________ macadamia nuts
13. ________ coconut
14. ________ cashews
15. ________ Brazil nuts
16. ________ peanuts
17. ________ sesame seeds
18. ________ chocolate
19. ________ coffee
20. ________ tea
21. ________ sugar
22. ________ vanilla
23. ________ paprika
24. ________ cinnamon
25. ________ chili powder
26. ________ black pepper
27. ________ lemons
28. ________ mangoes
29. ________ pineapples
30. ________ potatoes
31. ________ tangerines
32. ________ yams
33. ________ limes
34. ________ grapefruit
35. ________ oranges
36. ________ avocados

NAME ____________________ DATE ____________

LOGGING SOLUTIONS

THE "WRITE" STUFF

Trees provide oxygen for humans and animals to breathe, shelter for many species of animals, and homes for people. Cutting down large numbers of trees is potentially dangerous to our ecosystem. However, many people depend on the logging industry for jobs to support their families. Most of us use wood products, such as paper towels, paper cups, and newspapers, daily. Without the logging industry, we would not have many of these conveniences.

Use science books, magazines, or the Internet to research the different methods of logging. Research the pros and cons of each type of method. Try to see the issue from both sides—the perspective of environmentalists and the perspective of the logging industry. Think of several solutions to resolve their differences. Compile your information into a letter to the editor of your local newspaper, describing some possible compromises for both sides of this issue. You may include your own perspective since you probably use wood products every day.

LIFE SCIENCE

FOLLOW THE TRAIL SAMPLE EXPERIMENT

QUESTION: How does the height of an obstacle blocking a scent trail laid down by a foraging insect affect the number of foraging insects that can follow the trail?

HYPOTHESIS: If the height of an obstacle blocking a scent trail laid down by a foraging insect affects the number of foraging insects that can follow the trail, then the greater the height of the obstacle, the fewer the number of insects that can follow the trail.

VARIABLES, CONTROL, AND CONSTANTS:

Independent variable: Height of the obstacle blocking a scent trail

Dependent variable: Number of insects that follow an obstructed scent trail

Control: A scent trail that is unobstructed

Constants: Variables that must remain the same

- type/amount of food used as bait
- distance of bait from anthill
- material used to create obstacle
- width/length of obstacle
- method of measurement
- measurement tools

MATERIALS:

- outdoor location with anthills or colonies
- 10 cups (2.37 L) of moist sandbox sand
- 4 tbsp (59.1 mL) of peanut butter
- 4 microscope slides
- ruler
- 4 index cards
- plastic knife
- stopwatch
- measuring spoons

PROCEDURE

1. Place 1 tbsp (14.78 mL) of peanut butter on each microscope slide. Use the plastic knife to spread the peanut butter over the entire surface of the slide. This creates a larger feeding area, which will accommodate more ants.
2. Locate an anthill or colony.
3. Use the ruler to measure 8" (20.32 cm) from the anthill and place an index card on this spot. Label this index card *Path 1*. Place one microscope slide with peanut butter on the index card.
4. Repeat step 3 for the three remaining sides of the anthill. Label the index cards *Path 2*, *Path 3*, and *Path 4*.
5. As the first ants find each slide, use the moist sand to build a sand obstacle in the middle of the ants' original path between the anthill and the microscope slide. For each obstacle, the length of 4" (10.16 cm) and width of 1" (2.54 cm) should remain constant. The height of each obstacle will vary as follows:

   Path 1: height of 1" (2.54 cm)
   Path 2: height of 2" (5.08 cm)
   Path 3: height of 3" (7.62 cm)
   Path 4: no sand obstacle
6. Observe the ants for 30 minutes. Count the number of ants that successfully navigate around the obstacle for each scent trail. Record data on the data table.

NAME______________________________ DATE______________

FOLLOW THE TRAIL

EXPERIMENTAL DESIGN

Have you ever watched an ant colony at work? If you watch closely, you will notice that each ant seems to have a specific job, whether it is locating food or burrowing in the anthill. An individual ant could not survive without the rest of its colony; the ants all depend on each other.

In this activity, you will spend time observing ants. As ants search for food, they lay down a scent trail. Ants use this scent trail to lead other ants from the colony to food sources. Then, the ants work together to return the food to the colony.

TASK: Design an experiment to determine if ants can follow a scent trail that becomes blocked by an obstacle. Complete the worksheets (pages 10–14) as you design and perform your Follow the Trail experiment.

HINTS

HYPOTHESIS:

- Think about what you already know about ants from observing them in the colony. You may want to research what kind of food ants like to eat, as well as how they create their scent trails.

VARIABLES, CONTROL, AND CONSTANTS:

- What will you test?
- What will change as a result of the independent variable?
- To which trial will you compare all of the results?
- Which parts of the experiment must stay the same?

GRAPH:

- Create a graph that shows a picture of the data you collected in this experiment. Remember to label both axes and give the graph an appropriate title.

LIFE SCIENCE

MEET DR. JOHN WESTBROOK

SPOTLIGHT ON SCIENTISTS

Dr. John Westbrook is a **research scientist** for the Areawide Pest Management Research Unit at the United States Department of Agriculture. Although his degree is in meteorology, he does not just study the weather. He uses his background knowledge to find out how the weather affects different populations of organisms.

One of Dr. Westbrook's interests is the effects of weather on the growth and flight of insects that attack crops. He uses special weather balloons to track the winds that help insects quickly fly long distances. He has also studied the winter survival of insect populations in Texas and the high-altitude flights of insects and bats from Mexico to Texas. Dr. Westbrook enjoys working with scientists from other fields including entomology, engineering, and chemistry to help solve problems and protect crops.

When humans grow plants for food, such as corn, lettuce, and tomatoes, some insects will feed on these plants. Although the insects depend on these plants as a food source, they are considered pests to humans. The insects cause damage to the plants and make them unsuitable for humans to eat.

There are many types of insects pests that cause damage to crops. Use science books, encyclopedias, or the Internet to research an insect pest from the list below. Then, design a poster to present to your class that includes the required information.

- aphids
- leaf miners
- root maggots
- whiteflies
- cabbage worms
- grasshoppers
- parasitic wasps
- thrips
- cabbage loopers
- corn earworms
- tomato hornworms
- wireworms
- nematodes
- cutworms
- pickle worms

REQUIRED INFORMATION

- Description of the insect pest
- Types of crops the insect pest eats
- Type of damage the insect pest causes to crops
- How weather affects the insect pests
- What farmers can do to prevent these insect pests from damaging crops

LIFE SCIENCE

NAME________________________ DATE____________

DEDUCTIVE REASONING

SCIENCE SKILLS

Scientists can use **deductive reasoning** to solve problems that at first appear to be complex. Deductive reasoning helps solve problems through the process of elimination. To practice your deductive reasoning skills, complete the problems below.

PROBLEM 1: Using the following clues and deductive reasoning, find which student bought each kind of snack. Use the data table below to organize the facts. When you think you can eliminate a possible answer, place an X in that box.

There are four students at the snack machine—Uma, Kate, Juan, and Jack. They each decide to buy a different kind of snack—licorice, jelly beans, a granola bar, and potato chips.

1. The student who bought the licorice is a boy.
2. Kate is allergic to nuts in the granola.
3. A boy bought the potato chips.
4. Jack enjoys salty snacks.

Type of Food	Uma	Kate	Juan	Jack
Licorice				
Jelly Beans				
Granola Bar				
Potato Chips				

PROBLEM 2: Use the clues and deductive reasoning to determine the grade level and pet choice of each child. On another piece of paper, use the table from Problem 1 as a model to create a data table to organize the facts. When you think you can eliminate a possible answer, place an X in that box.

There are four cousins at a family picnic—Julie, Nate, Liz, and Anne. Each cousin is in school. One is in first grade, one is in fourth grade, and two are in sixth grade. They each own different pets—a hermit crab, a dog, a snake, and a parrot.

1. Julie and Liz are twins.
2. Nate is learning to read simple words.
3. The youngest cousin is allergic to animals with fur.
4. Anne's pet is a reptile.
5. Both Julie and Liz have pets that can make noise.
6. Liz does not have a mammal for a pet.

LIFE SCIENCE

NAME ______________________________ DATE ____________

EARS AND ADAPTATIONS

SCIENCE SKILLS

Many animals have special and unique adaptations that help them to survive. Bats have large ears that help them to fly and catch prey in total darkness. While in flight, a bat uses a series of high-pitched squeaks that echo off nearby objects—bushes, fences, branches, insects, etc.—and bounce back to the bat's ears.

In this activity, you will use **deductive reasoning** skills to make predictions about the adaptations of different kinds of animal ears. First, make a prediction about how the size, shape, and movement of each animal's ears pictured below is a beneficial adaptation. Then, use science books, encyclopedias, or the Internet to research if your prediction for each adaptation is correct. Write the answers to your research on another piece of paper.

Gray Wolf

Prediction: ______________________________

____

____

____

Bald Eagle

Prediction: ______________________________

____

____

____

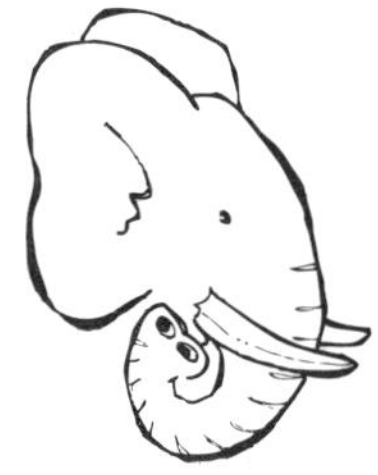

African Elephant

Prediction: ______________________________

____

____

____

Snowshoe Rabbit

Prediction: ______________________________

____

____

____

PEPPERED MOTH ADAPTATION

ENGINEERING CHALLENGE

Many animals use **camouflage** to hide themselves from predators. For example, before 1750, most peppered moths were white with black spots; this coloring camouflaged them against the white bark of the birch trees where they rested. However, during the Industrial Revolution, soot from the smokestacks of factories turned the bark of the birch trees from white to black. The light-colored peppered moths were not camouflaged on the dark, soot covered trees, and many were eaten by birds. The moths that survived had darker coloration, which camouflaged them against the darker tree trunks. Over time, these moths reproduced. Now, most peppered moths are dark with white spots. This is an example of an animal's adaptation to its environment.

CHALLENGE: Use the materials listed below to construct a model of a peppered moth that will be camouflaged in a chosen area of the classroom.

MATERIALS:

- clean soft drink bottles and cans
- clean yogurt containers
- cardboard paper towel tubes
- resealable plastic bags
- paper plates
- yarn or string
- clothespins
- aluminum foil
- paper plates
- colorful pencils, markers, and crayons
- paint
- any additional teacher-approved materials

GUIDELINES

1. Choose an area of the classroom.
2. Use the pattern below as a guide to create your peppered moth.
3. Decorate the moth so that it is camouflaged in the chosen area. Then, display the moth in that area.
4. Then, have several volunteers come into your classroom. How many camouflaged moths can they spot?

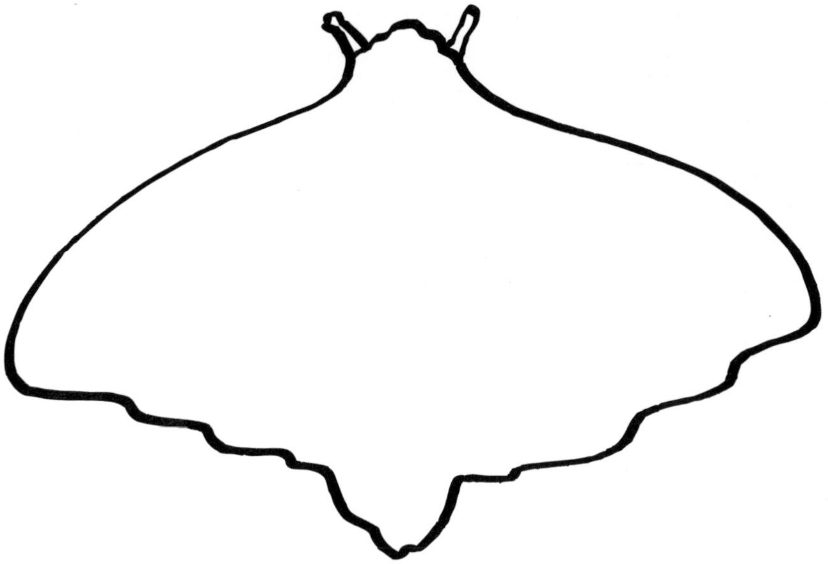

NAME_______________________________DATE__________

NAME THAT ADAPTATION

JUST THE FACTS

All animals have special adaptations that help them survive in the wild. Choose three animals from those pictured below. Use science books, encyclopedias, or the Internet to research the special adaptations these animals have that help them survive. Record your research below.

Skunk

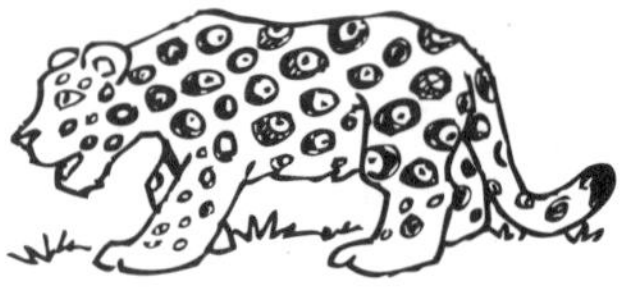
Jaguar

Great White Shark

Bat

King Cobra

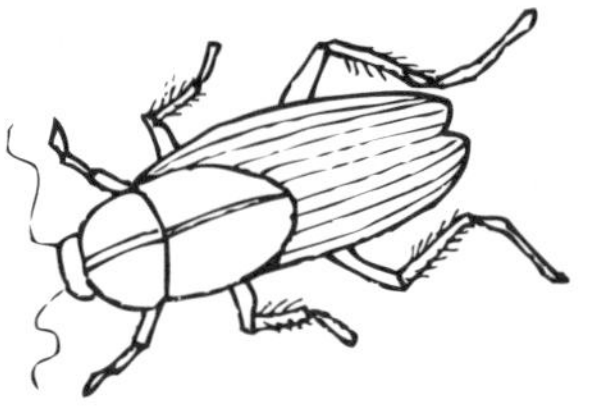
Cockroach

1. Name of organism:________________________________

   Adaptation:________________________________

   ____

   ____

2. Name of organism:________________________________

   Adaptation:________________________________

   ____

   ____

3. Name of organism:________________________________

   Adaptation:________________________________

   ____

   ____

ANIMAL ACTIVITY LEVEL SAMPLE EXPERIMENT

QUESTION: How does the time of day affect an organism's activity level?

HYPOTHESIS: If the time of day affects the number of that organism that can be collected, then greater numbers of nocturnal organisms can be collected at night.

VARIABLES, CONTROL, AND CONSTANTS:

Independent variable: Time of day (day or night)

Dependent variable: Number of organisms collected at each time of day

Control: Number of organisms collected during daylight hours

Constants: Variables that must remain the same

- type of collection device
- location where organisms are collected
- time of day and night organisms are collected
- technique for collecting organisms

MATERIALS:

- clothesline
- electric lantern or portable black light
- white bed sheet
- flashlight
- sweep net
- forceps
- collection jar and lid with air holes

PROCEDURE

1. Choose an outdoor location that can be easily accessed during the day and at night. This is where the moth population will be surveyed. Choose an open area with at least two trees, away from strong light sources. If necessary, use a flashlight at night to find the way to the location. Turn it off when you have reached the location.
2. String clothesline between two trees and drape the bed sheet over it.
3. Place the light source behind the sheet and turn it on. Wait quietly for the moths to be attracted to the light.
4. When a moth lands on the sheet, carefully capture it with forceps or the sweep net. Place the moth in the jar. Close the lid of the jar.
5. Repeat step 4 for 15 minutes. Record the number of moths collected on the data table.
6. Then, release all of the moths from the collection jar.
7. Repeat steps 2–6 in the same area and at the same time each day and night for five days. After five days and nights, find the average number of moths collected during the day and the average number of moths collected at night.

NAME________________________________DATE____________

ANIMAL ACTIVITY LEVELS

EXPERIMENTAL DESIGN

Did you know that most animals are adapted for survival? Consider the fact that a jackrabbit is built for speed, while a wolf is equipped with an excellent sense of smell. A turtle is adapted for survival by carrying its shelter for protection, while a bee can protect itself and its hive with its sting. Some animals that are **nocturnal** sleep during the day and are awake at night. They may have gained this adaptation to avoid predators that are active during the day.

TASK: Design an experiment to determine if an animal's activity level is greater during the day or the night. Complete the worksheets (pages 10–14) as you design and perform your Animal Activity Levels experiment.

HINTS

HYPOTHESIS:

- Think about what you already know about the animal you chose. Use science books, encyclopedias, or the Internet to research this animal's adaptations for survival.

VARIABLES, CONTROL, AND CONSTANTS:

- What will you test?
- What will change as a result of the independent variable?
- To which trial will you compare all of the results?
- Which parts of the experiment must stay the same?

GRAPH:

- Create a graph that shows a picture of the data you collected in this experiment. Remember to label both axes and give the graph an appropriate title.

NAME____DATE________________

MUTUALISM

JUST THE FACTS

Often in nature, organisms depend on each other for survival. Some organisms, such as lions and zebras, maintain predator-prey relationships. Others, such as ticks and dogs, maintain parasite-host relationships. While these relationships provide a benefit for only one of the organisms, sometimes organisms work together to the benefit of both. This is called **mutualism**.

Write each letter in the correct blank to match the animal on the left with its mutualistic partner on the right.

1. _______ **Clown fish**–eats parasites that feed on its partner's tentacles
2. _______ **Oxpecker**–perches on its partner and alerts it to the presence of predators
3. _______ **Hornbill**–flies near its partner and provides a warning call when predators are near
4. _______ **Egyptian plover**–feeds on the remnants of food between its partner's teeth and blood-sucking leeches around its partner's gums

a. **Nile crocodile**–opens its mouth and provides a food source for its partner

b. **Antelope**–provides a food source for its partner by allowing it to eat insect pests that are living in the antelope's hair

c. **Dwarf mongoose**–chases its prey out of the woods and high grasses; it shares this prey with its partner.

d. **Sea anemone**–provides its partner, which is immune to the sting of the anemone, with shelter and protection from predators.

Write the names of the animals in each mutualistic pair on the lines under each picture below.

5.

____

____

6.

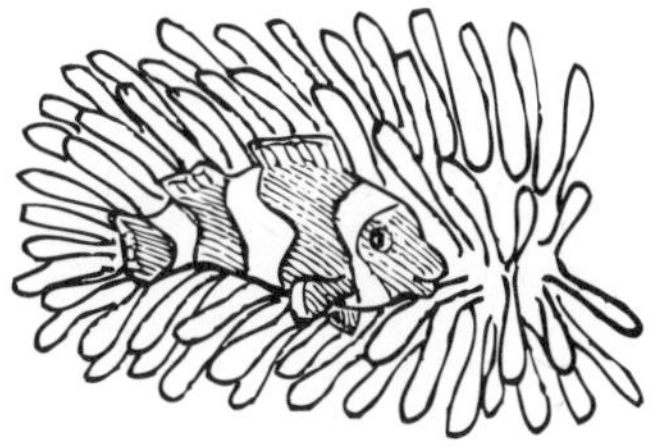

____

____

7.

____

____

8.

____

____

LIFE SCIENCE

NAME________________________________DATE____________

HUMAN IMPACT ON ANIMAL SPECIES

THE "WRITE" STUFF

Human activities can have a negative effect on many species of animals. What may seem like a small action, such as littering or cutting down several trees, can cause unseen problems for many animals.

Choose one of the mutualistic relationships between two animals from the Mutualism activity (page 121) or research to find your own example of a mutualistic animal relationship. Imagine that due to human activity, one of the animals in this relationship is threatened with extinction. Write a letter to the company or individual creating the impact and explain why it is important to save this animal. Discuss the effect of its extinction on the other animal in the mutualistic relationship.

LIFE SCIENCE

MEET VAUGHN WEAVER

SPOTLIGHT ON SCIENTISTS

In most households, after water used for cleaning and drinking is washed down the drain, it is sent to a water treatment plant. But, most people do not realize that this treated water may have an effect on populations of fish and other animals in the body of water where it is eventually released.

Vaughn Weaver is a **population ecologist** for the water department in Wichita, Kansas. His job as a population ecologist is to work with the local community to study how water from sewage treatment plants affects the plants and animals in the Arkansas River. He studies the current conditions of the habitat and writes a report that other scientists can read and compare to future reports.

At a very young age, Mr. Weaver knew he wanted to work with animals. He enjoys being outdoors, exploring the rivers and streams, and watching the wildlife around him.

Mr. Weaver tries very hard to teach as many people as he can about the importance of improving water quality. Since the actions of people in the past affect our present-day environment, we know that our actions will affect the environment of people in the future.

Did you know that the water you drink might come from a river or lake in your area? Many people do not realize that the water coming from the tap may be the same water in which they swim, boat, and fish! The water you drink goes through a very efficient cleaning process in order to remove dirt, bacteria, and harmful chemicals. To understand how difficult it is to provide water that is clean enough to drink, complete the following activity.

MATERIALS:

- sludge water (water with sand, gravel, small sticks, food coloring, coffee grounds, etc.)
- plastic foam cups
- rubber bands
- any additional teacher-approved materials
- cheesecloth
- coffee filters
- plastic containers
- paper towels

GUIDELINES

1. Brainstorm with your group to create a design for a filter that will clean the sludge water. Your filter design should make the water as clean as possible.
2. Draw the design of the water filter in the box on page 124.
3. Use the materials listed above to construct the water filter. Then, filter a small amount of the sludge water.

NAME ______________________ DATE ____________

Draw the design of the water filter in the box below.

1. How well did the design filter the water?

2. If water from the drinking fountain looked like the filtered water, would you feel comfortable drinking it? Why or why not?

3. Look at the filtered water through a microscope or magnifying glass. Do you see anything that might not have been trapped by the filter?

4. What are some things that a water treatment plant must filter besides dirt and rocks? Why might it be difficult to filter these things?

TRY THIS! How could you improve the design of the water filter? On another piece of paper, write a materials list and procedure for creating an improved filter and repeat the experiment.

LIFE SCIENCE

Observing Polymers (page 18)

1.–8. Answers will vary.

Polymer Pond Creatures (page 19)

Answers will vary.

Create Your Own Polymers (page 20)

1.–3. Answers will vary.

Solutes and Solvents (page 22)

1. The fastest way to dissolve the chocolate is chewing.
2. Chewing increases the surface area of the chocolate, making it easier to dissolve.
3. solute–chocolate candy
   solvent–saliva
4. a. solute–salt
      solvent–water
   b. solute–carbon dioxide and sugar
      solvent–water
   c. solute–chocolate syrup
      solvent–milk
   d. solute–coffee grounds
      solvent–water

Meet Dana Hamilton (page 25)

1.–10. Answers will vary.

Oil and Water Don't Mix! (page 26)

Answers will vary.

Reading and Making Graphs (page 27)

1. 10 m
2. airplane 1
3. four
4. airplane 4
5. three minutes
6. five minutes
7. 140 beats per minute
8. 140 beats per minute

Reading and Making Graphs (page 28)

Data Set 1:

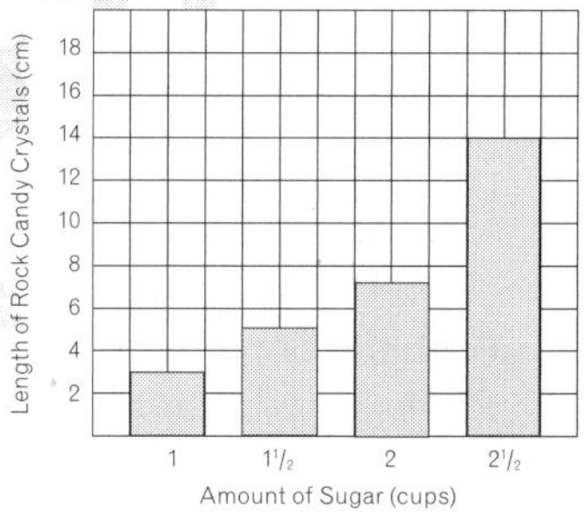

Data Set 2:

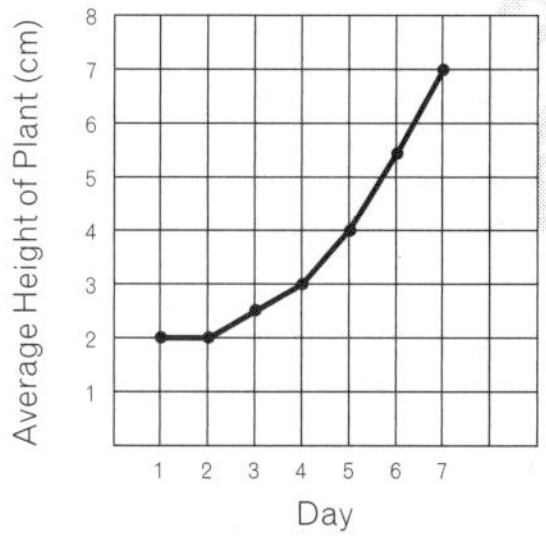

Newton's First Law (page 29)

1. Answers will vary.
2. Answers will vary.
3. The hovercraft has more inertia when it is moving since it has a tendency to keep moving while "floating" on a cushion of air.
4. the bottom of the CD and the table
5. There is less friction between the hovercraft and the table when it is moving since a cushion of air is created between the hovercraft and the table and less friction is created.

Newton's Third Law (page 32)

Answers will vary.

Highway Crash Cushions (page 33)

Answers will vary.

Newton's Balloon Cars (page 37)

Answers will vary but should include a description of Newton's three laws of motion and references to the activities from pages 29–36.

Force and Motion Crossword (page 38)

ACROSS

1. mass	3. Newton
4. third	6. propulsion
7. friction	8. inertia
9. acceleration	

DOWN

1. motion	2. second
5. first	7. force

Meet Todd Barber (page 39)

Answers will vary.

The Metric System (page 40)

1. 230	2. 1
3. 3.54	4. 500
5. 5	6. 0.6783
7. 0.03426	8. 67
9. 1,000	10. 0.0124
11. 2	12. 1
13. 0.01	14. 5,620
15. 0.2362	16. 3.6
17. 4.581	18. 25

Conductors and Insulators (page 42)

a. C	b. I	c. C	d. I
e. I	f. C	g. I	h. C
i. I	j. I		

k. Answers will vary.

l. Answers will vary.

1. A conductor allowed the current to complete the circuit, and the lightbulb lit. An insulator stopped the current, and the lightbulb did not light.
2. Most conductors are made of metal and have hard surfaces.
3. Insulators have softer surfaces and may be made of fibers, rubber, plastic, or wax.

Nuclear Power (page 45)

Answers will vary.

Downhill Fun (page 48)

1. potential
2. kinetic
3. Answers will vary.
4. Answers will vary.

More Downhill Fun (page 50)

1. The additional mass from the quarters increases the rate that the checker slides down the slope.
2. The fan simulates a strong wind. The electric fan produces wind that decreases the kinetic energy of the checker.

Types of Energy (page 51)

1. mechanical	2. radiant
3. electrical	4. thermal
5. nuclear	6. chemical
7. chemical	8. thermal
9. electrical	10. mechanical
11. radiant	12. nuclear

Rocks and Minerals (page 57)

1. metamorphic	2. mineral
3. sedimentary	4. igneous
5. sedimentary	6. igneous
7. mineral	8. mineral
9. metamorphic	10. sedimentary
11. metamorphic	12. sedimentary
13. igneous	14. igneous
15. mineral	16. metamorphic
17. mineral	18. mineral
19. igneous	20. mineral

Trip to the Center of Earth (page 58)

Answers will vary.

Gold Rush! (page 59)

1.–5. Answers will vary.

Meet Brian Fisher (page 64)

1. The colorful powder leached and spread throughout the surrounding sand in the glass dish.

Meet Brian Fisher (continued)

2. As water enters and mixes with the soil, it carries the powder (pollutants) with it and spreads it throughout the soil.
3. Answers will vary.

Digging for the Past (page 65)

1.–3. Answers will vary.

Problem Solving (page 66)

1. This activity is similar to the work of a paleontologist because he may only find small pieces of entire skeletons. He has to guess what the entire animal might look like.

2.–3. Answers will vary.

If Fossils Could Talk! (page 67)

Answers will vary but may include the following responses:

Woolly Mammoth Skull

- It resembles a modern day elephant's skull.
- It may have been a mammal, lived on land, and eaten plants.

Fish Skeleton

- It resembles a modern day fish skeleton.
- It might have lived in either saltwater or freshwater.

Bird Footprints

- Based on the size of the prints, the bird that them was most likely small.
- The climate in which the bird lived might be determined by dating rocks in the area.

Triceratops Skull

- This dinosaur skull has horns and plated helmet, which may have been used for protection.
- The lack of large teeth indicates that it may have eaten plants.
- It may have been a reptile.
- The crack in its skull might be from a fight with another dinosaur.

Hurricane House (page 68)

1.–2. Answers will vary.

Pangaea Puzzle (page 69)

Meet Dr. Gretchen Jones (page 72)

1. Students who track the "pollen" around the room and to other areas in the school represent animals or insects. Taking the pollen to another "country" could mean finding it somewhere outside the classroom (such as in the hallway, another classroom, or the cafeteria).
2. A palynologist should be familiar with pollen from all over the world in order to identify the source of any pollen that came from different locations.

Mission Measurement (page 73)

1.–2. Answers will vary.

3. This is similar to what engineers at NASA might experience because they need to make accurate measurements and calculations. Scientists need to work together to achieve their goals. It is different because a mistake made by NASA may put people's lives in danger and cost millions of dollars.

Out of This World Vocabulary (page 75)

1. e	2. h	3. f	4. a
5. i	6. j	7. b	8. d
9. c	10. g		

Planetary Exploration (page 76)

Answers will vary.

Martian Landing Gear (page 77)

1.–2. Answers will vary.

Earth and Moon Crossword (page 80)

ACROSS

2. elliptical
7. rotation
9. year
11. new moon
12. revolution
13. waxing
14. full moon
15. solar eclipse

DOWN

1. maria
3. lunar eclipse
4. day
5. tilt
6. sphere
8. waning
10. equinox

Future Space Missions? (page 81)

Answers will vary.

Meet Dr. Rosaly Lopes (page 83)

1. The color of play dough at the bottom of the straw was deposited first, while the color at the top of the straw was the last layer deposited.
2. Depending on how the volcano erupted (each eruption is random), the lava may not have flowed over the same areas. Therefore, the lava layers would not be evenly distributed.
3. Taking only one core sample would not allow scientists to understand the entire region. They need more data in order to draw good conclusions about the area's history.
4. Answers will vary.

Controls and Variables (page 86)

Answers will vary but may include the following responses.

Experiment 1:

Procedure:

1. Gather four of the same type of plant.
2. Talk to three of the plants and measure their heights each day.

Controls and Variables (continued)

3. After several days, calculate the average height of the plants.

Control: the plant that will not be talked to

Variable: talking to three plants

Constants:

- type of pot
- type of soil
- amount of water
- sunny location

Experiment 2:

Procedure:

1. Place a rubber band in a pot of water and heat the water.
2. Measure the water temperature with a thermometer.
3. Remove the rubber band at different temperatures and stretch it over a ruler.

Control: a rubber band stretched at room temperature.

Variable: the different temperatures

Constants:

- rubber band size, type, and manufacturer
- thermometer
- amount of water
- ruler

Experiment 3:

Procedure:

1. Gather three shoe boxes. Place the three crickets in separate shoe boxes.
2. Record the number of times each cricket chirps in a set amount of time.
3. Calculate the average number of chirps.
4. Place the crickets in the same shoe box and record the number of times the crickets chirp in a set amount of time.

Control: the trials when crickets are in separate shoe boxes

Variable: placing crickets together in the same box

Controls and Variables (continued)

Constants:

- crickets
- size of shoe box
- amount of time for each observation
- room temperature

Spread of Disease (page 88)

1.–2. Answers will vary.

3. The illness was passed from person to person as people "shook hands."
4. Answers will vary.

Growing Bacteria (page 89)

1. Answers will vary.
2. Different cotton swabs are used to avoid contaminating each sample with the sample taken before it.

Cellular Crossword (page 92)

ACROSS

2. Golgi bodies
4. chloroplast
5. DNA
9. cell membrane
10. lysosome

DOWN

1. mitochondria
3. cytoplasm
6. nucleus
7. cell wall
8. vacuole

Comparing Cells (page 94)

Diagrams will vary but should include the major differences between plants and animal cells.

Create a Mechanical Arm (page 95)

Answers will vary.

Observing Animal Behavior (page 97)

Answers will vary.

Observation vs. Assumption (page 98)

1. O	2. A	3. A	4. O
5. A	6. O	7. O	8. A
9. O	10. A	11. O	12. A
13. O	14. O	15. A	16. A
17. O	18. A	19. A	20. O

Animal Intelligence (page 101)

Answers will vary.

Animal Defenses (page 102)

Answers will vary.

Zoo Pros and Cons (page 105)

Answers will vary.

Meet Dr. Patrick Gannon (page 106)

Answers will vary.

Classifying Animals (page 108)

African lion–vertebrate; carnivore; warm-blooded

Praying mantis–invertebrate; carnivore; cold-blooded

Human–vertebrate; omnivore; warm-blooded

Striped bass–vertebrate; omnivore; cold-blooded

Bald eagle–vertebrate; carnivore; warm-blooded

Cobra–vertebrate; carnivore; cold-blooded

Grasshopper–invertebrate; herbivore; cold-blooded

Grizzly bear–vertebrate; omnivore; warm-blooded

Design a Closed Ecosystem (page 109)

Answers will vary.

Rain Forest Products (page 110)

Answers will vary.

Logging Solutions (page 111)

Answers will vary.

Deductive Reasoning (page 115)

Problem 1:

	Uma	Kate	Juan	Jack
Licorice	X	X	O	X
Jelly Beans	X	O	X	X
Granola Bar	O	X	X	X
Potato Chips	X	X	X	O

Problem 2:

	Julie	Nate	Liz	Anne
Grade	Sixth	First	Sixth	Fourth
Crab	X	O	X	X
Dog	O	X	X	X
Snake	X	X	X	O
Parrot	X	X	O	X

Ears and Adaptations (page 116)

Gray wolf–Ears are "cupped" for better hearing. They can be swiveled in different directions to listen for danger and prey.

Bald eagle–Ears are internal (inside of the body) to cut down on wind resistance and increase aerodynamics when flying at high speeds. Eagles use their sense of sight to find prey, rather than their sense of hearing.

African elephant–Large ears are loaded with small blood vessels. As the hot blood travels through the elephants' ears, it makes contact with the air, which causes heat to dissipate. Fanning the ears speeds up the cooling process.

Snowshoe rabbit–Ears are large for better hearing; they can be swiveled in different directions to listen for predators.

Name That Adaptation (page 118)

Answers will vary but may include the following responses:

Skunk–sprays its enemies to deter them from attacking

Jaguar–runs at very high speeds to catch prey

Great white shark–moves swiftly through the water; can smell injured prey from long distances

Name That Adaptation (continued)

Bat–uses sonar to find insect prey and navigate while flying

King cobra–"puffs" its head to make itself appear larger when threatened

Cockroach–hard outer covering (exoskeleton) protects it from predators

Mutualism (page 121)

1. d 2. b 3. c 4. a

5. Nile crocodile and Egyptian plover
6. Sea anemone and clown fish
7. Dwarf mongoose and hornbill
8. Antelope and oxpecker

Human Impact of Animal Species (page 122)

Answers may vary.

Meet Vaughn Weaver (page 124)

1.–3. Answers may vary.

4. Microorganisms, such as bacteria, are often found in water sent to water treatment plants. It would be hard to filter these organisms because they are very small. Chemicals are often used to destroy them.